THE JAPANESE SOCIAL STRUCTURE

THE JAPANESE SOCIAL STRUCTURE

Its Evolution in the Modern Century

Second Edition

TADASHI FUKUTAKE

Translated and with a Foreword by
RONALD P. DORE

UNIVERSITY OF TOKYO PRESS

Translated from the Japanese original NIHON SHAKAI NO KŌZŌ
(University of Tokyo Press, 1981)

© 1989 by UNIVERSITY OF TOKYO PRESS
First edition published 1982. Second edition 1989.
ISBN 4–13–057016–1
ISBN 0–86008–446–9

94 93   5 4 3
Printed in Japan

CONTENTS

CONTENTS

TABLES

FOREWORD

Perhaps it is a measure of the importance attached to age hierarchy in Japan that the Japanese like to classify people by the generation they belong to—the prewar generation, the postwar generation, etc. By that reckoning Professor Fukutake belongs to the "wartime generation," the men and women who came to maturity in the early 1940s and were young enough and vigorous enough, and sufficiently untainted by the decisions which carried Japan into its disastrous war, to become leaders of the second Japanese Enlightenment. He rapidly emerged as the leading interpreter among professional sociologists of what it could and should mean for Japan to be transformed into a democratic society. His most concentrated efforts went into his field studies. As he tramped the villages of every region of Japan with his notebook and his ready smile and his ability to exchange farmers' jokes, he was concerned to tease out the delicate interrelationships between kin-solidarity and patriarchal domination, between benevolent patronage and exploitation, between neighborly closeness and suppression of individuality, between the suppression of individuality in general and the suppression of the individuality of the poor in particular. In his more theoretical and polemical writings he examined Japanese society in the comparative perspective of the development of the West. And on the whole he did not like what he saw.

His ideal was clear. He wanted to see a Japan inhabited by autonomous, responsible, and public-spirited individuals. He wanted to preserve the strong and dutiful concern for the realm of the public which characterized prewar Japan too: he did not want to encourage the privatized concerns of those who are content with personal relations and the comforts of family life. But the focus of the public concern of the responsible citizen should be the welfare of individuals, not national glory. Loyal patriotism and submission to the authority of the nation's leaders should give way to a critical attitude toward authority and a lively concern with asserting the rights of the individual. Individuals should not be constrained and hemmed in by pressure from "primordial" groups—their patriarchal family, the tightknit beehive of the local neighborhood or village community— but they should *choose* to bind themselves—in farmer's cooperatives, in progressive political movements and (though less discussed) in marriage—in relations of cooperation with their fellow men rather than relations of competition.

Such, roughly, was the ideal which Professor Fukutake shared with a good many other intellectuals and social scientists in those heady days of the immediate postwar period when the slogans of democracy echoed from one end of the political spectrum to the other. Japan, as he saw it, was a long way from exemplifying that ideal: democratic rights granted to an acquiescent public as a benevolent act by the head of an occupying army—human rights as part of a constitutional package deal handed down from on high— were not the same as, could not have the same meaning as, human rights won by the determination and cooperative solidarity of like-minded individuals determined to resist oppression. But all was not lost: the rights prescribed in abstract were still denied in the concrete. In the family, in the workplace, in schools, men and women were still required to suppress their individualities in the interests of "harmony," supposedly in the interests of the group as a whole; often, in fact, in the interests of the privileged ones who dominated the group. It was still possible, through education and exhortation, to establish these rights for real, in a struggle which consolidated them, making them truly rights which had been won.

Thirty years later, the Japan in which men dreamed of individual autonomy and argued about the meaning of liberty and modernity—with holes in their shoes and hunger barely appeased by squash from their tiny back gardens and noodles made from American relief wheat—that Japan has gone forever. And for some of Professor Fukutake's contemporaries, too, the ideals of that time have been replaced with others more, perhaps, "in keeping" with the glass and stainless steel of the office blocks and the marble halls of the banks and luxury restaurants which typify modern Japan.

But he himself remains unshaken in his convictions and unmoved in his concerns. If any reader, bemused by the torrent of "interpretations" of Japanese society by Japanese scholars now filling the glossies which pour from the presses of the Tokyo business and official PR establishment, and dazzled by the new hot gospellers of Quality Circles and the Japanese Way of Life who are taking over the American business schools, should think that Japan is now seized of a mood of self-confidence, an urge proudly to reassert its national traditions and to deny that its society is less than perfect, then he will find Professor Fukutake an interesting corrective. For his view of affluent Japan is still a distinctly jaundiced one. He acknowledges, of course, the enormous material gains that have been made. He acknowledges the extent to which the old constraining bonds of the family and the neighborhood community have been loosened to give the individual more elbow room, more space to breathe:

the old *ie* system survives, he notes, in little more than an imprecisely defined belief that the eldest son should carry on the family, and in patterns of residence which are as much a function of housing shortage as of ideology. But in the place of former abuses he finds new ones: the mindlessness of the mass media, the loss of a sense of responsible citizenship as "the public" becomes the mass of mass society and as a critical attitude toward social institutions gives way to apathy and support for the status quo. Meanwhile an unshakable Establishment of businessmen and conservative politicians carries the country further along the path of economic growth, neglecting expenditure on social infrastructure and giving only inadequate attention to social welfare and social security. And the atomized individuals of the new cities have failed to create a new sense of "community" (and note his recording of the new word *komyuniti* to differentiate this new community springing from individual fraternal commitment from the inherited primordial bonds of the traditional *kyōdōtai*). Until they do, apathy and indifference will leave all the abuses intact.

But I have concentrated too long, in this foreword, on the message, when many readers will be buying the book for the medium in which it is carried—the lucid descriptive account of the evolution of Japanese society since the middle of the nineteenth century which it is, after all, Professor Fukutake's main purpose to provide. And they will not be disappointed. Professor Fukutake has a gift for mapping the outlines of a social structure—be it the prewar family, the typical village community, the relations of trade unions and political parties, or the national class structure—with an unusual clarity and pertinent use of statistics. The transformation of samurai into bureaucrats and businessmen, the growth of tenancy in prewar villages, floor space or welfare expenditure per person, the number of households linked to a main sewer, the proportion of the population who think they are middle class; the information is there, tellingly deployed in his succinct thematic chapters.

To me, of course, the message remains the most interesting. I suppose there was a time, more than thirty years ago, when he first let me accompany him on village research trips and taught me all I know about villages, when I agreed with all he said—or at least did not dare to disagree. Since then, as our friendship has matured, we have come to appreciate, and even savor, the differences of opinion that add spice to our relationship.

Some of our differences are about concepts (it *does* seem to me that there is a nasty trade-off to be made between individual liberty and community solidarity that one cannot evade by distinguishing between old bad community and new type good community) and some are about relative evaluations. I cannot think, for example, that Japanese government policy has been quite as neglectful of the social infrastructure as he suggests. On the day I write this I hear a British Minister of the Environment on the radio evasively trying to explain why he cannot hope, even by 1985, to imitate Japan's action of nearly a decade ago and ban car engines that require leaded petrol—without actually giving the reason that the British motor industry will not stand for it. I consequently find it hard to agree that (as governments go) the Japanese government has been shamefully neglectful of the social environment in its single-minded concern with "production."

But Professor Fukutake needs sticks to beat his government with as I need sticks for mine. And Japanese politics and politicians, to be sure, are hardly the paragons of rational enlightenment whom I would want to defend from Professor Fukutake (though I might go into battle for the bureaucrats on occasion). I wish, though, that Professor Fukutake would not go on assuming that the *proper* place for an effective opposition to develop is in the way the

Marxian paradigm says it should—through a Socialist party based on a militantly class-conscious industrial working class. I wish he would look more closely at the potential political role of the new "intellectual proletariat"—not forgetting its student vanguard who have been responsible for the most strident expressions of political feeling in recent years (whose stridency, after all, nearly robbed Professor Fukutake of his health when he was for many months, such was the degree of personal trust which he enjoyed on all sides, in the center of the maelstrom as a principal negotiator with student militants in a turbulent University of Tokyo).

Not that this perception helps *me* to make any intelligent prognosis about the future of Japanese society, any more than it would or should change Professor Fukutake's main judgments. It is a measure of the scope of his analysis, and of the breadth of sympathies which underlie it, that no possibilities are dogmatically foreclosed. Readers will learn an enormous amount from this book about the astonishing transformations of Japanese society over the last century: they will learn essential facts about the structure of that society today. They will also learn a good deal about its author, a scholar of subtle understanding and generous sympathies, of humanity and charm.

Ronald Dore

February 1982

PREFACE TO THE SECOND EDITION

The original Japanese edition of this book (1981) was expanded from the text I wrote to accompany my 25–part lecture series televised by the Japan Broacasting Corporation (NHK) in 1980–81. My dear friend Ronald Dore kindly agreed to undertake the English translation and, despite his very busy schedule, began translating from the galley proofs, even before the original was published. The English edition thus appeared in the following year, 1982.

Besides this English translation, two other translations appeared in 1982: a Korean edition and a Chinese edition; and in 1985 a second Chinese edition was published in Taipei. This English edition went into several printings, and also from hardcover to paperback. As the author, I am deeply honored to have so many readers worldwide.

On the occasion of this second edition, I have sought to update the data as far as possible. The updated statistics incorporated in the second Japanese-language edition (1987) and, where available, more recent data have been used.

In the seven years since this translation was first published, Japanese society has undergone many changes, particularly in the context of stable economic growth. On the political scene, recent tax reforms and the exposure of political corruption have brought about unprecedented popular political awareness. We are witnessing protests and demands for reforms as never before. Nevertheless, the information and analysis presented in this book are still valid in their description of the society.

The day will eventually come when this book will be outdated and rendered useless, but until that day comes, it is my sincere wish that as many readers abroad as possible will read and use this book to reach an understanding of Japanese society today.

May 1989

Tadashi Fukutake

THE JAPANESE SOCIAL STRUCTURE

PREFACE TO THE FIRST EDITION

This book is based on a series of broadcast lectures which grew out of a course I gave in the General Studies division of the University of Tokyo in the early 1970s. The turmoil of the "events" at the university and a period of illness which followed had made it impossible for me to continue the fieldwork-based study of rural society which had been my special concern throughout most of my career. This provided the opportunity to revert to the theme which had preoccupied me in the immediate postwar period (Fukutake, 1948, 1952) and which I had only occasionally tried to tackle since (Fukutake, 1960, 1972, 1981)—the overall analysis of where Japan had come from and where it was going: the question of the democratization and modernization of Japanese society.

I began my career as a sociologist with wartime studies of Chinese society. China, for all that we speak of it as a country of the "same race, same script," has a social structure different from Japan. It seemed to me that I came to understand Japanese society the better for my opportunity to see it in comparison with China. Later, my interest in comparative sociology was further stimulated by a two-month stay in India at the end of 1960, followed by a six-week study of Indian villages, two years later, in company with economist and social anthropologist colleagues Ōuchi Tsutomu and Nakane Chie. These experiences convinced me that Japan, which the nineteenth-century intellectuals said ought to "withdraw from Asia and join Europe," never was a typically Asian society in the first place. I published reports of these comparative studies in both English and Japanese (Fukutake, 1967, 1969) in which I argued that structural differences in the family and village community were related to the overall social differences between China, India, and Japan. It is my belief that the family and the village community provide a key for the understanding of Japanese society, and that perspective is an important one for these lectures. It is a perspective particularly essential for the understanding of prewar society. The extent to which these special characteristics of that society have disappeared or still remain is a question which needs to be asked in the analysis of postwar society too.

In these original lectures I referred to prewar and postwar Japan as "modern Japan" (*kindai*) and "contemporary Japan" (*gendai*), though in this translation, to avoid confusion, I shall use the words "prewar" and "postwar." At any rate, the defeat of 1945 really does mark a watershed, a change in the nature of Japanese society which requires a clear recognition. What is often, in the industrialization dimension, spoken of as the difference between an industrial society and an advanced industrial society is also part of the prewar/postwar difference. A word is necessary, in this context, about the concept "modernization." Some feel that it is vague and ambiguous and that "industrialization" is better. Certainly the concrete content of modernization amounts to industrialization, plus the urbanization that accompanies it—the steady growth of mechanized manufacturing production and the relative decline of agricultural production as a proportion of the national product, and the changing relative importance of agricultural and

4

urban areas. These are visible phenomena, and the question whether or not as a consequence of these structural changes "premodern" men and social relations are transformed into "modern" men and social relations is, although in the nature of the case a difficult one to answer conclusively, a question of some importance. The fact that in postwar Japan the question of the modernization of the society was hotly debated precisely as the problem of the *democratization* of Japanese society is sometimes explained (Tominaga, 1973) as a consequence of the fact that the prewar society was brought down in ruins by a reckless war and intellectuals were assailed by a sense of original sin because they had been unable to stop that war. Whatever the motives, the discussion itself—and the problem of democratization and its relation to modernization—seems to me a very serious one.

Hence in the first part of these lectures I want to look at the process of modernization since 1868, the date of the Meiji Restoration—under what conditions and at what point in world history it unfolded, and what was its basic character. Subsequently Japan's industrial structure went through many changes, but in general, although one might want to qualify the statement somewhat for the late 1930s when the nation was put on a war footing, the prewar period as a whole, in spite of the progress of industrialization, saw a Japanese social structure dominated by peasant households and family enterprises in both manufacturing and commerce. In such a social structure the family, the village, and the urban neighborhood were important elements, and first of all the role which the family—the *ie*—system played in the development of Japanese society, for better and for worse, needs explication. Next follows a discussion of the community-like nature of the village and the small town and urban neighborhood. In this context "community" does not refer to what the social and economic historians call a *Gemeinde,* but rather a *Gemeinschaft:* that is to say, a society which is relatively self-sufficient in satisfying the needs and desires of its members in everyday life, a "community of fate" which circumscribes the lives of most of its members from the cradle to the grave. Consequently emotional bonds of union and harmony transcend in importance those which depend on rational calculation of interest. The community contains, too, clearly ranked status distinctions among its members, and this helps to enforce social constraints, thus producing not only relations of dominance between superior and inferior, but also relations of mutual assistance. The villages and urban neighborhoods of prewar Japan were of this kind.

The social character of the Japanese was formed in families, villages, and neighborhoods of this type: it was a familistic society. By "familistic" I mean a society in which the individual cannot stand alone apart from his family, and in which the family as a whole is considered much more important than its individual members; also a society in which these family relations are extended to relations beyond the family itself. "Familism" is the pattern of behavior and social relations, and the value system which characterize such a society. It is commonly found in agricultural societies organized into peasant family units. There is a special characteristic of the Japanese version, however, which the author once named "feudal familism." At the end of the first section I shall explain how that kind of feudalism became intertwined with the class structure to make of Japanese society as a whole a familistic society, and how it was this which led to the disaster of the "Great Japanese Empire."

Part Two begins with a discussion of the process of democratization after that disaster, and of the limits of that process. The public opinion polls about democracy conducted since the war have generally found about 60 percent of respondents agreeing that "democratic ideas should be modified in accordance with the realities of Japan." That is approximately what happened. The slogan of the 1870s, "Enrich the country, strengthen the army" was modified: the second half was forgotten and all energies were concentrated on enriching the country in the period of very rapid economic growth that followed. I then go on to examine the social changes of the postwar period during the decades of high growth: how rapid industrialization was attained, how the agricultural structure was transformed in consequence, how rapidly urbanization took place and with it the increase in the number of wage and salary employees —and how the lives of those employees changed as they came to constitute an overwhelming majority—and how the mass society which thereby developed differs from the society of the prewar period. We shall see how as a consequence of these changes the *ie* system so integral to the structure of prewar society, though still leaving discernible traces, very largely disappeared. The local community of the village and small town also changed and lost its community character.

Table 1   Opinions on Postwar Democratization

Year	Postwar democratization needs further strengthening	Important to amend aspects unsuitable to Japan	Other; Don't know
1955	21	64	15
1965	23	54	24
1975	16	57	27

Sources: For 1955 and 1965, surveys by the Prime Minister's Office; for 1975, by NHK.

Contemporary Japan, the product of all this social change, is the subject of the third section. It begins with a discussion of how far Japan and the Japanese of today differ

7

from the prewar period, and in what respects their character remains the same. Much use is made of opinion-poll
data for this purpose. Then I analyze the stratification system in comparison with the prewar period and go on to discuss how the postwar social structure has produced a paradoxical political structure in which the conservative parties
undertake "radical renewal" and the radical parties "conserve" what are, indeed, the factors which have sustained
conservative politics. Conservative politics have pushed
Japan forward into the ranks of the economic Great Powers,
but this economic Great Power has not only been unable
to cure imbalances within the production structure itself;
it has also neglected the imbalance between productive
capacity and the quality of daily life. Although "balanced
economic and social development" became the main slogan
on the billboards of successive cabinets toward the end of
the 1960s, those billboards slowly began to fade without
anything being really done. Today, social security and
social welfare, belatedly expanded as a spillover from the
period of high growth, are being reappraised as that epoch
comes to a close. They face a great problem as the aging of
the population becomes ever more marked. Thus Japanese
society has reached a major turning point. The lectures end
with the hope that we shall see the emergence of a new
basis for social community in the critical decade of the
1980s.

PART I

THE SOCIETY OF PREWAR JAPAN

CHAPTER 1

THE MODERNIZATION OF
JAPANESE SOCIETY

The Meiji Restoration of 1868 set Japanese society on the road to modernization. In the common schematic view of history, mankind progresses from primitive society to ancient society, from ancient society to feudal society, and then from feudal society to modern capitalism. This is, of course, not a progression which every society experiences, but Japan at least fits the model. It is clearly a society which had a feudal system, and a society which, with the Meiji Restoration, proceeded from that feudal state to become a modern capitalist society.

The modern society which developed is markedly different from that which preceded it. The anthropologist Robert Lowie has remarked that if we take the history of mankind hitherto as a hundred years, then for the first eighty-five years man was in nursery school. For the next ten he was in primary school. Secondary school, high school, and university have all been crowded into the final five years. It is a plausible analogy, so great was the leap which human society made from the medieval to the modern stage, and so dazzling the evolution of modern society itself.

The period has been one of leaping advance in productivity, accompanied by progress in transport and communications technology, which has expanded the social life-spheres of individuals and produced a society with an ever more complex social division of labor. In modern society fewer individuals live and die in the villages and towns in which they were born: more and more are geographically mobile as they seek their living elsewhere. They no longer are frozen in a social status accorded them at birth: the possibilities of rising or falling in the social scale increase. Man, as citizen, is freed from the local isolationism and the status discrimination of traditional society and ideally creates a society of free and equal individuals. Modern society is a society of citizens.

With these developments men and women who had been bound by the ties of status and of the local community come to see the complex intermingling of interpersonal relations in this expanded world as a "society." In Europe, too, it is after the beginning of the modern period that the words "society," "*Gesellschaft*," or "*société*" came into use. In Japan too, the word *shakai* came to be used for the first time in the early Meiji period as a translation of the word "society." (Fukuchi Gen'ichirō—known as Ōchi—is said to have used it first in 1875.) For the people of the Tokugawa period (1603–1868), although they were aware of the wider world, there had seemed no need to envisage the wider pattern of social relations, so difficult to grasp in its reach beyond their own village or neighborhood, as an abstract entity called a "society."

But did the society of modern Japan, which thus came to be consciously perceived *as* a society, thereafter develop normally as a citizen society, as a society of free citizens? That Japan's modernization was distorted, and that a citizen society failed to mature, has been frequently demonstrated, but if that was the case, why was it so? An important part of the answer lies in the fact that 1868, the starting point of Japan's modernization, was already about a century later than the British industrial revolution and the French revolution. Nor can one overlook the fact that the momentum was provided by the threatening appearance off the coast of Japan of "Black Ships" coming from the advanced countries.

At the end of the Tokugawa period the structure of Japanese feudal society had still not reached a sufficiently advanced stage of disintegration. It was, to be sure, disintegrating, but it had not reached the point of such general upheaval that it was ready to give birth to a modern capitalist society. The impoverishment of the peasantry and peasant revolts were fairly widespread phenomena, and were shaking the foundations of the system. But they were not yet on a nationwide scale, nor were they such as to challenge the existence of the feudal order itself. The commercial capitalism of the moneylenders was eroding the feudal economy to a certain extent, but the industrial capital capable of supporting a new modern society was still very much underdeveloped. In such an economy the family, the village, and the small town circumscribed the lives of the majority of the people within the confines of a tiny world; few were able to develop a consciousness of the wider society beyond the bounds of their small self-sufficient communities. Within the isolated universe of the village and the town the premodern forms of social life continued as before.

Consequently, when the isolation of Japan's feudal society was forcibly broken, and the country opened up to foreign intercourse as a result of outside pressure, the shock was devastating. As the advanced countries passed through the bourgeois revolution and matured as modern societies, their capitalism expanded into imperialism. Hence the pressures on Japan to open the country carried with them the danger of colonization.

The Meiji Restoration was a product of this one-century gap between Japanese history and world history. The distortions of Japan's modernization were due, more than to anything else, to the pressures which this gap created. That was why the Meji Restoration had to be carried out under the leadership of the lower-ranking samurai and through a coalition of the outer fiefs. And it explains why those lower samurai, as they switched from a policy of "expelling the barbarians" to one of "opening the country," felt that transition to be a national humiliation. Dedicated as they were to overcoming the contradictions of their feudal society, the lower samurai were still men of a feudal character; that was a part of them they could not deny. Almost instinctively they sought to perpetuate the traditional social structure within the modern society. *Meiji ishin* means, literally, the Meiji Renovation, but it was at the same time, as the standard English translation suggests, a Meiji "Restoration"—a restoration of imperial rule.

Thus from the very beginning the road taken by the restoration government distorted the path of modernization. The new political leaders, deeply conscious of the humiliation of being forced to open the country, and realizing how far Japan lagged behind the nations of Europe and North America, concentrated efforts on preserving Japan's independence in the face of the threat of colonialism, and building a nation strong enough to stand up against the Great Powers. Their objective was not to build up a modern citizen society; it was, rather, to "catch up," to go at one bound from feudalism to imperialism. Japan's modernization was modernization for national defense, for revision of the unequal treaties which had been forced on Japan by the Western powers, for the creation of a "wealthy country, strong army," as the dominant slogan of the time had it.

Thus, on the one hand, modern science and technology were welcomed as part of so-called Western civilization, and every effort was expended to foster modern industry. This was what people had in mind when they spoke of "the era of civilization and enlightenment" and of "enriching the country and strengthening the army." On the other hand, and simultaneously, the ideology of emperor worship was energetically propagated, the need to counter "Western techniques" with an "Eastern morality" was emphasized, and the morality of loyalty and filial piety was disseminated throughout the land. This "divine country" ideology served to check the growth of a self-conscious sense of citizenship such as modernization might have brought; it preserved feudal familism and taught the superiority of the Great Empire of Japan as a familistic state. The mass of the people, living out their lives in the tiny microcosms of their local communities and with no understanding of the true character of the modern state, were indoctrinated with an irrational pride in the uniqueness of the Yamato race, a recasting of the spirit of devotion and sacrifice which had been cultivated in the feudal society, now redirected toward the new Imperial state. This was not the kind of patriotism which could be made compatible with self-conscious individualism. It was essentially an emotional kind of patriotism which served as a bridge between local communities and the national community, in the absence of any general understanding of what the proper relation between the two should be.

These efforts, moreover, though they widened and deepened the contradictions, achieved a certain measure of success. A capitalist society was indeed built—if at the cost of sacrificing agriculture: the liberation of the peasantry, which is a precondition for a modern bourgeois revolution, was left incomplete. Capitalism made rapid advances thanks to the importation of modern science and technology and to generous government support and protection. The development of communications which accompanied the increase in productivity joined the disparate regions, for so long isolated units loosely held together in the feudal system, into a modern centralized state. One corner of backward Asia achieved a constitutional government of sorts and created a state equipped with a modern military machine. It was, to repeat, in comparison with the countries of Europe and America, a highly distorted form of modernization. Through the development of state enterprises and their subsequent selling off to private individuals—through the promotion of bureaucratic capitalism—the Japanese capitalist class acquired a "politico-merchant" character, growing in the embraces of, not in opposition to, the government. Developing as it did by utilizing feudal remnants within the society, Japanese capitalism never performed the historically progressive role which capitalism should perform—that of opening the way to liberty and equality. Hence, the creation of all the institutions characteristic of a modern state did not allow ideas of popular sovereignty to take root, nor promote the development of bourgeois democracy. The outward appearance of a modern state was obscured by the reality of a familistic state in which the Imperial Family claimed to be the original stem family of which all other families were supposedly branches.

Thus the process of modernization from above, carried forward with astonishing speed, was one which amplified the imbalances and distortions which the society originally contained. Relief from the pressures which resulted was sought overseas in policies of imperialist aggression. Instead of responding to the people's demands, following the path of democratization, and fostering the development of human freedom, all moves in any such direction were suppressed in plans for external expansion. And when these distortions reached breaking point, the Great Japanese Fmpire could not but disintegrate. The tragedy of a Pacific War was the final reckoning of these accumulated contradictions.

CHAPTER 2

THE INDUSTRIAL STRUCTURE OF PREWAR JAPAN

The industrialization of Japan which began with the Meiji Restoration was swiftly carried forward at the initiative of the government. Having in the 1870s carried through its program of dismantling the feudal system, the government went on to the modernization of transport, communications, the currency, and the financial system and at the same time promoted the transplanting of modern industry in the form of state enterprises. The financial basis for these industrial promotion policies was provided by tax income from the reformed land taxation system. At a time when there was very little economic activity outside of agriculture, the taxes paid by farmers, who made up as much as 80 percent of the working population, provided the overwhelming bulk of government revenue. A tax levy which was approximately equal in its incidence to the dues of the feudal period was available to be devoted to the fostering of manufacturing.

The capitalist industrialization thus promoted centered at first around the textile industry; later, in the twentieth century, shipbuilding, armaments, and other heavy industrial production also became important.

Nevertheless, in spite of these rapid developments, Japan at the end of the Meiji period, in the first decade of this

PREWAR JAPAN

Table 2   Employed Population by Industry

Industry	1907	1930
Agriculture	61.7	47.8
Fisheries	1.9	1.9
Mining	1.1	1.1
Manufacturing	15.1	19.9
Transport	2.2	3.9
Commerce	9.5	16.6
Public and other services	4.4	5.9

Sources: For 1907, Yamada, 1957, p. 152; for 1930, National Census.

century, was still an agricultural country. As Table 2 shows, the agricultural population in 1907 was still estimated at 62 percent of the total. Manufacturing still employed only 15 percent. Moreover, within this manufacturing workforce, employees in firms with more than five workers, including all the state enterprises, numbered only about 22 percent of the total. The vast majority in the small backyard factories and craft workships were self-employed workers and their family dependents. Hence, even with 15 percent of the working population in manufacturing, probably not more than 5 percent were wage employees of a modern type (Ōuchi, 1962).

Add to this the fact that of the workers in the larger establishments with five or more workers, the majority were women, and men made up only 40 percent of the total—a consequence of the concentration of activity in the textile industries. Even if the shipyards and ordnance factories and other state enterprises are added to the total, males still made up only 44 percent. Given that the majority of the female workers were transients working only for a few years before marriage, it will be obvious that, even after forty years of modernization, the development of a modern work force was extremely slow and Japan was a society overwhelmingly dominated by peasant and small family enterprise.

18

In the second and third decades of the century, capitalist modernization accelerated. What had been, in 1910, an agricultural country, in which the agricultural 60 percent of the population produced 50 percent of the national product, was transformed into an industrial Japan. The proportion of the national product originating in agriculture and forestry fell below 30 percent, and the production of factory industry increased from less than 30 to 55 percent. Light industry continued to develop, but there was also a growth of steel production and shipbuilding, and new developments in the machinery, chemical, and electrical industries. Workers in establishments with more than 500 employees, which had made up less than 20 percent of the total five-or-more-employee establishments in 1907, came to exceed 30 percent twenty years later.

Even so the 1930 census showed the agricultural population still close to a half of the total work force, while the industrial population had barely reached 30 percent. And wage workers who conformed to the usual industrialization stereotype—those in the larger establishments with five or more employees—made up about a third of all those in manufacturing. Thus, in spite of a considerable increase since the first decade of the century, wage workers still accounted for roughly only one-tenth of the working population. Even sixty years after the Meiji Restoration, Japan was a society heavily dominated by peasant and family enterprise. Table 2 shows a big increase in numbers employed in commerce between 1907 and 1930, but here again employers and the self-employed outnumbered their subordinate workers (even including family workers), and tiny family enterprises predominated to an even greater extent than in manufacturing.

It is worth remarking, however, that by this time more than half of those employed in factories with five or more employees were in factories with at least 100 workers. Because of the predominance of the textile industry the sex ratio was still about 50 percent, but there had been an increase in large factories, particularly in the heavy and chemical engineering sector, dominated by the *zaibatsu* enterprises. Here there was a growth of a modern blue-collar labor force, but they were still not the majority; particularly among males, over 60 percent of factory workers were in tiny establishments with four or fewer workers. There was a dualism in the structure of the manufacturing labor force: in spite of the growth of modern industry, the pre-modern relationship between the *oyakata* master craftsman and his journeyman was still partially preserved.

Table 3 Factory Workers by Size of Establishment (percent)

Year	Size of establishment						
	5–10	–30	–50	–100	–500	–1000	1000–
1909	13.6	21.3	9.5	12.3	22.5	7.0	13.8
1919	8.6	16.4	8.6	11.2	23.7	9.2	22.3
1929	10.8	15.6	8.1	10.5	23.8	11.2	20.0

Source: Kōjō Tōkei-hyō [Factory Statistics].

Subsequently the Japanese economy moved rapidly on to a war footing. Industrialization, with an emphasis on the heavy and chemical industries, proceeded at an accelerated rate. In about ten years the agricultural population had declined to close to 40 percent and the industrial was approaching 30 percent. Workers in establishments with over 500 workers reached 60 percent of the factory labor force, and employees 40 percent of the working population. But all this was a short-term consequence of the concentration on military procurement and hardly has to be taken into account when characterizing the structure of prewar Japan in general.

Industrialization naturally brought urbanization in its wake. Around 1870, when agriculture occupied 80 percent of the population, the towns contained something less than 10 percent. Even if one includes all towns with more than 10,000 population, they numbered only 99 and contained less than one-tenth of the nation's citizens. By the same criteria, there were 166 urban settlements twenty years later with 15 percent of the population and by 1920, when the first census was held, 232 with 32 percent. If one takes only those areas administratively defined as cities, however, their proportion of the population was less than 20 percent in 1920 and still under 25 percent—in 99 cities—in 1930. Table 4 shows that it was still less than 25 percent if one takes "administrative areas with more than 50,000 population" as the criterion.

Table 4   Population in Urban Areas (percent)

Size of urban area	1920	1930	1940
1,000,000+	6.2	7.1	7.2
500,000+	2.2	4.8	2.7
100,000+	3.8	6.1	9.5
50,000+	3.7	6.8	5.2
Total	15.9	24.8	34.6

Source: National Census.

The urban population increased rapidly with a subsequent growth of heavy and chemical manufacturing and by 1940, 125 cities contained 38 percent of the population, a figure which increased to 40 percent just before the end of the war—again due to special circumstances; the 25 percent urban population of the 1930s is a more characteristic figure of the prewar period. And one must remember that this urban population, even though one quarter of the total, still contained a majority of workers in petty commercial and manufacturing family enterprises.

Thus, though becoming the only industrial society in Asia, Japan had not lost its agrarian characteristics. In

21

spite of rapid urbanization, it was still a rural society as a whole. To put it another way, in spite of modernization, the majority of the constituent members of that modern society were either in peasant households cultivating tiny plots of land or were workers in commercial or craft enterprises who, albeit that their numbers were increasing, were still predominantly self-employed and family workers in enterprises not markedly different from those of the pre-modern period.

Both for peasants and for these urban small-enterprise workers, the family was at one and the same time both a living unit and a producing unit. Agriculture, or commerce, or their craft was for them "a family business." It was a business which, in principle, the eldest son of each generation would naturally inherit. The traditional *ie* system retained its great importance in modern society.

It is also important that the farmers, who remained in the majority until the 1930s, lived by cultivating their ancestral lands in small rural settlements. In these settlements the constraints of the community were binding; they were little microcosms within which the bulk of people's life activities were encompassed. Although villagers were drawn into the money economy and increasingly subject to the buffetings of the market, it was within the village that the network of social relations which made up their lives was most densely multiplex.

For those in the tiny family enterprises of the cities, too, the shop was at the same time generally the house; the living quarters were often in a corner of the factory. Most of them, like the farmers, spent their nights and days within the confines of a single neighborhood. The neighborhood organizations which had existed in the premodern period were resurrected as the *chōnaikai,* and ties within the neighborhood were strong. Theirs was much more a village-like

22

than an urban social life. This was true even in the capital city of Greater Tokyo, in the older *shitamachi* areas.

Hence, for an understanding of the society of premodern Japan, we must first look at the *ie*, the traditional form of the family, and at the *mura*—as Japanese social scientists have come designate, not just the village which was the word's original meaning, but also village-like communities in cities and work organizations.

CHAPTER 3

THE IE SYSTEM: MERITS AND DEMERITS

It was the basic principle of the Japanese family that the eldest son (or the eldest daughter where there were no sons) brought his bride (or her groom) into his (or her) home and the young couple settled down to live in the same household with parents and grandparents. The axial relationship of such a family was not the marital relationship but the parent-child relationship, and this lineal (agnatic) family with strong, partiarchal authority constituted the basic building unit of Japanese society.

The family in this lineal system was not just a group of cohabiting kin, but also an *ie*. The actual group of living family members were seen as only the epiphenomenal representation of the *ie* which existed through time, uniting ancestors to descendants in direct continuity provided by its lineal genealogy. Younger sons in each generation might split off to form their own new *ie*, each of which thereafter continued to perpetuate itself as a "branch family" of the original "main family," in exactly the same lineal way. It was generally the eldest son who carried on the family and succeeded to the position of family head, and with his succession to the headship he usually succeeded also to the family property and family business—or at least he had first claim so to succeed. Younger sons might receive portions of the family property when they established branch families, and so might daughters when they went out of the family to marry, but they did not have any right to demand such a portion, and the emphasis placed on the continuance of a strong main family was such that their portion was generally a small one.

This pattern of primogeniture inheritance was the concentrated expression of the *ie* system and can be regarded as a product of the feudal social structure. As Max Weber (1924) pointed out, the purest forms of feudalism were established in Europe and Japan, and it was feudal experience that gave Japan an inheritance system favoring elder sons, rather different from the partible male inheritance systems of China and India. In the Tokugawa period the hereditary stipend of the samurai family was passed on intact to the eldest son. For farmers, artisans, and merchants, division of the family property was not impossible. Feudal regulations did limit the division of agricultural land below a certain acreage in order to preserve the tax-paying capacity of farm units, but in practice younger-son branch families could be created. Nevertheless, the samurai inheritance system was sufficiently well adapted to the desire of commoners to maintain their family property and the vigor of their family business for it to influence their inheritance system too.

This traditional inheritance system was not only preserved by the Meiji government, but actually strengthened. The Meiji Civil Code took the samurai institutions as the basis for its family provisions. There had been regions in Japan where ultimogeniture prevailed—the elder sons gradually left the parental family until only one was left. Again, in regions of low productivity, families in which the birth of a son was delayed would recruit a groom for the eldest daughter and allow her and her husband to succeed. But with the Meiji Civil Code primogeniture became the law of the land. Whereas the French Revolution's ideals of liberty and equality were expressed in the Napoleonic Code's provisions for equal inheritance of all children, modern Japan, a few decades later, compromised with realities in giving recognition to a premodern inheritance system.

This *ie* system had a good deal to do with the industrialization of Japan after the Meiji period. Japan's rapid industrialization, as foreign scholars have noted, owed a good deal to the cultural capital accumulated in the fief schools and the popular *terakoya* schools of the Tokugawa period, and to the spread of compulsory education after the Meiji Restoration (Dore, 1964), but if Japan, like China and India, had been a country which gave equal inheritance shares to younger sons, it might not have been able to ensure the steady supply of labor necessary for industrialization. As long as there were new labor markets to receive them, the younger sons who were not destined to inherit the family headship and property—irrespective of social stratum—took positive steps to leave the family and seek a livelihood elsewhere. And they could do so assured that their natural family would accept an obligation to take care of them if they fell on hard times, the more so because their departure had enabled the family property to be kept intact. This permitted a considerable saving in social welfare expenditure in the course of Japan's industrialization.

Again the *ie* system meant that, as compared with the system of divided inheritance, family status remained relatively stable. Although the status system of the Tokugawa period was officially abandoned, status consciousness long persisted, and, indeed, the formal distinction between aristocrats (*kazoku*), samurai (*shizoku*) and commoners (*heimin*) was still preserved at least on the family registers. Even in the Tokugawa period the boundaries between statuses had been very loose compared with, say, an Indian

27

caste system. After the Meiji Restoration even those loose status boundaries were set aside with the declaration that the "four orders are equal." The opportunity was there and the desire to rise in the world—to "raise the family name"—was strong, the more so because status *consciousness* remained powerful. This again was a factor favorable to industrialization.

However, appropriate as it was in economic terms for the promotion of industrialization, in social terms the *ie* system was a strongly negative factor, operating to delay social policy legislation, keeping wages low and work conditions harsh, and preventing any demand for social welfare services from becoming powerfully articulated. And, as we shall see later, the *ie* system was directly related to the bankruptcy of the imperial family state—itself an extension of the *ie*. All in all, the defects of the system balanced its virtues.

The word *ie*, as we have already seen, stood for a concept which transcended the idea of a "family" as a group of presently living individuals. It was conceived as including the house and property, the resources for carrying on the family occupation, and the graves in which the ancestors were buried, as a unity stretching from the distant past to the present and occupying a certain position in the status system of the village or the town. The *ie* in that sense was far more important than the individuals who were at any one time living members of it, and it was seen as natural that the individual personalities of family members should be ignored and sacrificed if necessary for the good of the whole.

Given the emphasis on direct lineal continuity, it is not surprising that considerable power attached to the household who carried on the line of descent. The strength of the household's powers derived from his many functions: he was in charge of the family property (which was seen as

the property of the *ie* and not of the househead as an individual), he played the central role in the rites for the
ancestors, and he directed the labor of family members in
the family business. The proceeds of the family business all
went into the househead's purse. The labor contribution of
individual family members would have been hard to cal-
culate within the work of the family as a whole, but in any
case the question of individual incomes did not arise; it
was the family which earned income from the farm or
shop or workshop which it ran as a family business, with
the family property as the means of production. The househead who controlled this income consequently had full
powers over the family's consumption. The househead's
wife would take care of small matters of everyday expenditure from money which her husband vouchsafed her, but
all expenditures out of the ordinary needed the househead's
approval. It was he who provided pocket money for the
other members of the household as needed.

Thus the position of househead was always one of great
power both in production and in consumption. But it was
not one of absolute power. It was only in the wealthier
houses of some antiquity, of the kind which might have a
written "family constitution" laid down by some earlier
househead, not in ordinary peasant or shop-keeping families, that there was any special emphasis on the authority
of the househead. But he was nevertheless generally the
central authority figure, as was symbolized in northern
Japan by customs governing who sat where. In those areas
the main living room always had a square *irori* open hearth.
One side of the hearth, called the *yokoza,* was always reserved
for the househead—even in families of low status in the
community. These poorer families did not have the material basis of property ownership to reinforce *ie* consciousness,
and so they did not develop the sort of authoritarian househead control common in the upper status families. But

even in poor families, their very poverty required close unity, required the members of the family to cooperate, and required individuals to subordinate their own interests to those of the *ie*. And it was the househead's will which was likely to prevail in deciding on any important matters what the interests of the *ie* were.

Given a lineal family system which gave such importance to the househead, it was natural that the status of the eldest son, destined to be the next househead, would also be high. There was a phrase which neatly summed up the ideal family: "one to sell, one to take over, one to stand by." The daughter, ideally born first, was the one to be "sold off"—married out of the family. Then came the eldest son, and because one could never feel secure, because the eldest son might die young, one needed at least another son as a standby. In general, the oldest son was treated differently from his younger brothers—as a much more important person. This was especially so in the poorer and more backward areas of northern Japan where eldest sons were called *ani* and younger sons *oji*, and the latter were clearly seen as standbys. Even in other areas where the distinction was not quite so sharp, the eldest son was called *sōryō* or *oyakata*, and the younger sons got the rawest deal: they "had to eat cold rice." There is no reason to suppose that on a personal level younger sons were any less lovable to their parents, but the categorical imperative of family continuity dictated that the "successor" son should have a higher status than his brothers. He was not only the one who would eventually succeed as househead; it was also on him that would devolve the total responsibility of caring for the househead and his wife in their old age.

By contrast daughters were inessential to their families. The fact that the daughter comes first in the proverb just cited simply indicates that daughters, who are likely to be born with a fifty-fifty probability anyway, are best born first so that they can help with the housework when their siblings are growing up. In a male-oriented *ie* system it required considerable expenditure to provision a girl for marrying off, and even after marriage the family might have to supply clothes and pocket money in order to help her standing in the new family. That was why no one wanted to have a large number of girls. In the poorest families, however, there was little question of spending large sums of money on daughters. There they were rather seen as potential workers who would later go out to earn low wages as cotton operatives or domestic servants. In the very poorest families they would help their parents by very literally "selling themselves" into indentured prostitution. This was the family structure which produced the girl workers who gave the cotton industry its vital role in the industrialization of modern Japan.

In this way the *ie* system prevented human equality and created sexual discrimination within the families in which Japanese were born and brought up. It also created status distinctions between family units themselves—the ranking system of "main families" and the "branch families" which had split off from them. The groups of so-called *dōzoku*, made up of a central main family, branch families, and branch-branch families bound by mutually recognized links of genealogy, contained a certain basic element of master-servant subordination in the main-branch relation. So it was that fictive substitutes for true kin relations were possible, and a servant in one of the families of a *dōzoku* could become a quasi-family member and as such established eventually a branch family which then became a constituent unit of the *dōzoku*. Again, if the younger son of a branch family were to work for some time for the main family and receive a property portion from that family to establish a branch family, he would be counted in the group as a branch of that main family—not of the branch family in which he was born—with which, indeed, his family would henceforth enjoy equal status. The Japanese *dōzoku* differed in certain features from the Chinese clan or the Indian *gotra*. When the ranking of main and branch families was reinforced by differences in economic power, the main family was able to exercise strong control over the other constituent families and the *dōzoku* kept its cohesion as a distinct unit. Whereas the Chinese clan preserved its unity thanks to the property of the whole clan, in Japan it was the family property of the main family which provided the material basis for the *dōzoku* unit.

It has to be pointed out, of course, that this kind of typical grouping was not general in modern Japan. But to some degree the superiority of main families in a main-branch relationship was widely recognized, and branch families were frequently in some respects dependent on, and in consequence constrained in their freedom of action by, *dōzuku* ties. Another extrapolation of the *ie* system was the tendency to create patron-client relations fictively modelled on the parent-child relationship—the so-called *oyabun-kobun* or *oyakata-kokata* relation. Just as the *dōzoku* group was an extrapolation of the Japanese *ie,* so the *oyakun-kobun* relationship was an exemplification of the key principle of Japanese familism: the equation of the parent-child relationship with a master-servant or leader-follower relationship. This kind of familism was a common axis of social cohesion in Japan, and as we shall see, it, too, as a principle of social organization, was a mixed blessing.

CHAPTER 4

VILLAGE AND TOWN AS COMMUNITY

We have already seen that at the time of the Meiji Restoration some 90 percent of the population lived in villages and more than 80 percent were engaged in agriculture. Even half a century later, in the mid-1920s, agriculture occupied half the population and urban residents had not yet reached a quarter of the total. In the interval there had been very little change—apart from minor fluctuations—in the absolute number of farm households and agricultural workers, so what had happened was a transfer to the cities of the natural increase in the rural population. And since rural fertility was approximately 50 percent higher, this inflow from rural areas steadily increased the town population. One consequence of this was that even around 1940 when the urban population was approaching 40 percent, eight out of every ten Japanese had been born and brought up in a village.

Hence the village was the mold in which the Japanese of modern times was formed. Kida (1956) calls the Japanese village "the substratum of Japanese culture," and although one may have doubts about his grasp of village structure, his title is not an exaggeration. A political scientist has sought to analyze the "mental structure" of modern Japan in terms of the principles of order of the natural village

(Kamishima, 1961), and the attention paid by many other scholars to the village and village society amply testifies to its importance in the understanding of modern Japan.

In the Tokugawa period, by and large, a single nucleated settlement formed a separate village—though there were sometimes exceptions when a small settlement would be incorporated into a neighboring larger one or a number of tiny clusters of houses in mountainous areas would be grouped together as a single village. Each village would have its "assessable yield," determined by a land survey, and annual taxes in kind had to be paid in accordance with that assessment as a collective responsibility of the village as a whole. The limits of the village and its fields were clearly demarcated so that when any villager cultivated land within a neighboring village's boundaries he paid his tax on that land through that neighboring village. Even today these village boundaries, although they have lost all administrative significance whatever, are still something that villagers are usually aware of: some scholars speak of villages having their own "sovereign territory." This is a particularly Japanese characteristic, not to be found in other Asian countries, such as China and India. One way of putting it is to say that membership in the village is a territorial rather than a social-relational definition, and this has served historically to reinforce "village consciousness."

A traditional village subsisted on irrigated rice agriculture requiring intensive input of labor. The actual creation of the rice fields and laying down of the irrigation system was the first prerequisite. Thereafter the maintenance of the irrigation system was not something that could be undertaken by an individual household; it inevitably required collective labor by the villagers as a whole group. Again, when the farmers relied on green fertilizer which they themselves supplied from the areas of hilly open space which were allocated to each village, village control over the use of these spaces was essential to sustain the production system. Those forested areas were also an important source of firewood, charcoal, and building timber. Communal control over the forest areas was as necessary as for water. The significance of the forests did tend to diminish in the modern period with the increased use of commercial fertilizer and the frequent subdivision of common forest land among individual households, but the irrigation system, even if it was refurbished under some national scheme, still continued to require cooperation from the villagers. Even if farming was mainly a system of private family production, the existence of resources over which the community had a monopoly made supplementation of individual by cooperative effort necessary. It is in that sense one can speak of Japanese villages, even in the modern period, as genuinely village "communities" of a corporate kind.

If agricultural production retained a number of community aspects, it is not surprising that village social life also had a community character. The farm households which made up village settlements became far more involved in the market economy after the Meiji Restoration than they had been before, but they still were for the most part engaged in grain production, and they still provided their own subsistence. In this sense, the villages still had something of a self-sufficient character and still were something like closed communities, little microcosms which circumscribed the production and consumption of most farmers. The communitarian element in agriculture extended itself to other spheres of life: to mutual assistance for weddings and funerals, to cooperative work in housebuilding and repair.

The unitary nature of the village was symbolized in the *ujigami,* the shrine of the protecting deity found in each village. The villagers' sense of membership in their community was enhanced too by the relative isolation of what

35

were generally nucleated settlements, and by the disputes which arose with neighboring villages over rights to water and forest land. In contact all day and every day with the same set of villagers, and bound to them by a wide multiplicity of ties, villagers could not but have a continuous awareness of "belonging" to the village. Given that most such villages consisted of two or three score of households, at the most not much more than a hundred, and that the life spheres of the villagers were largely encompassed within their boundaries, they interacted with each other on a basis of real intimacy. Each house in the village, moreover, because mobility was so low, bore a history stretching back into the past. A village community was, therefore, an accumulation of historical associations, between people who knew not only each other's present but each other's past as well. The importance of these complex and multiple interpersonal ties was further enhanced in a situation in which the basic productive activities of the household could not be carried on independently and arbitrarily, free of the constraints of the village community.

And that was not all. The Japanese village community is often spoken of as hierarchical in contradistinction to more "flat" village communities in the West. Community solidarity was certainly interwoven with the stratification system based on landownership. The villagers who could not survive without mutual help and communal labor had their role also in the landlord-tenant system and occupied a position in the status hierarchy which was based on it. In concrete terms, villagers were related not only by neighbor relations and kin relations, by gift exchange and by labor exchange, but also by ties based on the renting of land and on wage labor. For this reason, the constraints imposed by village society became tighter the closer one was to the bottom of the hierarchy. The poorest families at the bottom were, one might say, entirely "embedded" in the communitarian village.

There were, of course, very considerable changes in the community of the village as time wore on. Production for the market increased, and villagers' lives reached out further beyond the village boundaries, which ceased to circumscribe their vision. That part of their productive activity which required whole-village cooperation became of lesser proportional importance. More were able to find opportunities for by-employment outside the village. One important change in this regard was the local government system established in 1888 which amalgamated groups of four or five existing villages of the Tokugawa period into single units of administration. The new administrative villages were called "villages," and the old villages came to be called *buraku*, which is perhaps best translated as "hamlet." This change alone, transforming what had been a self-governing unit into a segment of a larger administrative village, represented a very great change indeed.

However, these new administrative villages were so preoccupied with the tasks imposed on them of carrying out the delegated functions of the modern Japanese state that they were not really able to take over the self-governing powers of the older villages. Effectively, the latter remained self-governing units and were simply utilized as administrative sub-units, required to subcontract some of the functions assigned to the administrative village. Attempts to combine the communal property of the separate former villages into the property of the new administrative villages, or to bring their protective gods together in a single village shrine, thereby molding the societies of the separate units into a single new village society, had very little success. In fact, eventually the move was rather the other way. As rural areas came to be shaken by tenancy disputes

37

in the 1920s, and as the situation was further aggravated by the depression of the 1930s, all the emphasis shifted to preserving the "pure customs and fine traditions" of the old-style village as the natural unit for neighborly assistance and rehabilitation through self-help. With the Villages Fit for an Empire Movement which developed during the war years, the bonds of the traditional village were drawn even tighter.

So, in spite of the variety of changes which took place in the villages as a result of Japan's modernization, the constraining power of the village community to paper over the contradictions of the village stratification system in the name of solidarity and harmony did not diminish. Numbers of new organizations were formed from the turn of the century—cooperatives, women's institutes, youth groups, and so on—but they all retained the principle of all traditional village organizations, namely that every villager in the eligible categories should automatically become a member. And the operations of these groups followed the same principle as traditional village meetings, namely that all decisions should be taken by unanimous agreement.

Compared with village communities of this kind, no one could argue that the *machi*, the ward neighborhoods of the urban areas, had the same community character. Nevertheless, the traditions of the Tokugawa town ward, with residents selecting ward officials, sharing out labor duties for the upkeep of the ward's roads and shrines, and deciding everything in ward meetings, still continued. In the older districts of the cities the old traditional patterns of the *gonin-gumi* ("five household groups" uniting the property owners and tenants in small neighborhood clusters) could still be found and still served to strengthen the organization of the ward as a whole. In the newer areas where the cities had spread out into the former countryside, the village settlements which had been engulfed continued their village

traditions, albeit in a changed form. The ward neighborhoods usually created their own new formal organizations
to promote harmony and friendly relations within the neighborhood. And in numerous respects these new neighborhood organizations resembled the *buraku* hamlets of rural
areas: membership was not membership of individuals,
but of households; all households became members automatically, or one might say semi-compulsorily; their functions were non-specific and spread over a wide range of
activities, and they came to be treated as subcontracting
units for the local administration. Such neighborhoods
would have a festival rather like the festival of the village
shrine, and neighborhoods predominantly inhabited by
self-employed craftsmen and shopkeepers had—though of
course the population was more mobile and lacked the
stability of the village—more of a village than an urban
character. When the German sociologist Tönnies (1887)
was drawing his distinction between *Gemeinschaft* and *Gesellschaft,* between community and association, he included
the medieval city, along with the family and the village, as
typical forms of *Gemeinschaft,* and one can justly say that
Japanese cities had those characteristics even into the modern period.

They were characteristics particularly marked in the
cities which had developed from former castle towns or
towns centered on great temples, but they were found equally in the new cities which had developed around large
new factories. The latter, even if they were genuinely industrial cities, were often places where the workers lived in
housing estates provided by the firm so that, interacting
with the same group of people both at home and at work,
they created a society which was rather like a village.
Where, with the development of such factories, commercial
centers sprang up and gradually changed a collection of villages into an urban community, the original inhabitants

tended to absorb newcomers into the framework of what remained a village-like society. In the suburbs which filled up with the houses of the new employees, the original villages were certainly urbanized, but here, too, the new employees tended to treat their place of residence as a mere "bedtown," and the neighborhood organizations which they were obliged to join were dominated by the original land-owners and family enterprises, very much as in traditional village. It often used to be said that even the great city of Tokyo was one great village, and exaggeration though that might be in any of the many senses the phrase could have, it nevertheless has a measure of truth. The microsocial character of prewar Japan, in both rural and urban areas, really was a structure of village and neighborhood units of such a tightly solidary character that talk of "one great village" does not seem entirely out of keeping. So much so that Japanese sociologists have taken to writing the word *mura,* the traditional word for "village," in phonetic script, rather than with the traditional Chinese character, as a term of art for that pattern of communitarian society which they see as the typical building block of the Japanese social structure, in both rural and urban areas.

CHAPTER 5

THE SOCIAL CHARACTER OF THE JAPANESE PEOPLE

It was in the *ie* and the *mura* described in the last two chapters that the personalities of the Japanese people were molded in the prewar period. Every child born into a Japanese family was brought up from the very beginning either as the eldest son who would inherit the family headship, or as a younger son who would have to make his own way in the world outside the family, or as a daughter destined to be married into another family. Each received a treatment which accorded to his prospective status. The idea of "doing things for the sake of the family," although it meant different things in concrete terms depending on one's social status, was still a universally compelling norm of family life. Being expected to conform to the expectations attaching to their position in the status order within the family, people learned to inhibit any personal desires which might go beyond the limits of what the family could tolerate or threaten its existence. However humanly natural such desires might be, if they did not fit the framework the family laid down they would have to be sacrified. The duty of obedience to the household, however unreasonable his commands might be, was enforced as the cardinal virtue of filial piety, the axis of family morality. Absolute obedience

41

served to preserve the harmony of the family, of which the household was the kingpin.

The constraints of a *mura*-like neighborhood society also had their effect. Parents, cramped by the need to keep up appearances and attend carefully to neighborly obligations (or *giri,* as this virtue was called), expected children to grow up accepting the established customary morality and to be careful not to breach it in all their dealings. Rather than teach them the difference between right and wrong and the need for autonomous self-regulated conduct, "Don't do that: people will laugh at you; you will lose face" became the basis of discipline. The development of ego control, of the capacity to act according to one's own judgments and carry through principles one personally believed in, was inhibited from infancy.

Growing up in such families, which, within the local village or neighborhood, each had their own status in the community stratification system, children were required to learn not only to observe their status within the family but also to observe the status of their family within the community in all their actions. The existence of this status-ranking order made parents look forward to the hope that children would move a step up the hierarchy, although upward social mobility was a remote possibility for the majority of children. I have already remarked that mobility aspirations led to a good deal of movement between statuses and that this contributed to Japan's economic growth, but the great majority of people were resigned to the fate which their birth offered them and sought to live in harmony, content with their status position.

Through primary school education, with its emphasis on the ethics course, these characteristics were reinforced as children were trained to take their place in society as loyal subjects. For those whose families had a farm or small retail or craft business, the residential community in which they lived had its own system of order to which they had to conform. They were required to act in conformity with their status and to restrain their egos out of respect for the community's need to maintain an atmosphere of harmony. Or, if they moved as employees into a workplace which had little connection with that local community, they had to conform to an atmosphere which took functional organizational hierarchies as hierarchies of personal quality. If they should make the mistake of treating other people as equals, they would find it hard to find a secure position in the workplace, much less to expect promotion. However just an argument one might want to put, however good a proposal one might want to make, if it would upset the harmony and disturb the status system of the workplace, it had to be suppressed if one wanted to avoid the criticism of superiors or of colleagues.

The underlying attitudes and principles of conduct of people brought up in this way in prewar Japan might be summed up in the two phrases "supremacy of custom" and "submission to authority." Behavior was for the most part guided and regulated not by internalized conscience or rational judgment, but rather by custom and authority. Another way of putting it is that the individual, living for harmony and status, lacked autonomy, the capacity for independent action.

That is to say that the emphasis on harmony leads to conformism in behavior. For a Japanese, the safest course was to tread the path of convention with everyone else. Consequently, whatever his reason or his conscience might tell him he should do, if doing it would invite isolation he would be unwilling to take the risk. Indeed, his very ability to react critically to conventional behavior was likely to be highly underdeveloped in the first place. And as the habit of conforming with the crowd and suppressing individuality grew, so the fear of isolation increased and lead to a deeply rooted traditional conservatism which disliked any change. "Avoiding initiatives," "not rocking the boat" were elevated to the status of principles of conduct. "No curses from gods you don't worship," as the proverb has it. Any change which required some positive reaction was ignored or evaded, and the recommended rule of conduct became: "If that's the way the world is, fine! Is that so, I did not know,"—in the words of an old saying—attitudes reinforced by the status order.

Behavior within such a status order was also, as another proverb had it, a matter of "wrapping up in something long"—adopting the passive safety-first practice of suppressing one's individuality and submitting obediently to the will of one's status superiors. Where men were always in some relationship of subordination and superordination to each other, the sense of inferiority toward one's superior could be compensated for by a sense of superiority toward one's own inferior. In the common injunction "look below you, not above you," subservience and arrogance appear as two sides of the same coin. There was no room here for consciousness of human rights, nor was there likely to be any outburst of indignation if rights were violated. The only sentiment likely to be prompted was a resentful sense of shame if one was not treated with due regard for one's proper status. The kind of personality fostered by this status consciousness and these authoritarian attitudes to life was the obedient follower and his counterpart, the ambitious status-seeker. And the consequence of making authoritarian control within a status system the guiding basis of life was on the one hand that men became unable to act without orders from on high, but on the other, in areas where authority could not reach, it led to a thoroughgoing tendency to "fiddle" things in one's own self-interest. This was most notably obvious in the world of the old prewar army, but at the same time it was characteristic of Japanese society as a whole—what the army considered as its hinterland.

Such behavior, in either case, is based on external, not on internal criteria. In that sense, Japanese morality may be called an exterior morality. A person was moved by what people around him would think: appearances and *giri* were of the first importance. Locked into the atmosphere of harmony which was typical of the isolated community, reliance on the noble customs of ingrained tradition, a keen sense of one's own status, and obedience to the commands of those in authority were the means of making one's way in the world. To criticize and resist the majority, or to argue with a superior and seek to set him right, was only likely to invite resentment and exclusion as an enemy of the established order. A more positive attitude, expressed in the attempt progressively to reform that order itself, was incompatible with an exterior morality. A truly mature person was someone who could suppress such positive initiatives and behave with a clear sense of status and occasion, and that was the sort of Japanese which the public education of the Imperial state sought to create.

As this kind of psychology becomes institutionalized and rationalized, it leads to a philosophy of life which one might call resigned realism—a set of fixed ideas taught by the realities of daily experience. Paradoxically, the logic of daily life in Japan was illogical. It lacked any idealism which might seek reform of society and opposed to it a realism in the worst sense. The world was not a place that could be run by reason; life was a matter of fate, and all one could do, it was thought, was to "leave it to luck; leave it to heaven." Those who acted without autonomy had to bow to "established facts" and rationalize their avoidance of responsibility on the grounds that they were forced to do so by surrounding circumstances. The availability of the excuse that "it was not my positive intention to do so" reveals the underlying psychology of Japanese social behavior—a logic of irresponsibility. For men who seek the criteria for their conduct outside themselves, and for whom there can be no question of showing resistance to those in authority above them, there can be no ethic of responsibility. And so, in the Imperial state whose whole structure turned on the single person of the emperor, the logic of irresponsibility applied even to the highest leaders. The evasion of responsibility for the war through the argument that no blame attached to the emperor, that it was his advisers and the military who were at fault, was seen as perfectly compatible with the argument that *they*, the advisers, were also forced to act the way they did by their situation, that they were only following orders, that the responsibility must lie in the surrounding circumstances. And so from the highest to the lowest local levels the leaders were able to swagger their way through history. In the Imperial state of modern Japan, every chief and leader was a petty emperor to his own group, devoid of any true sense of subjective responsibility for his own conduct. And by the same token, their followers and subordinates, while outwardly obeying and conforming to their wishes, did not give them positive willed support. This automatically exaggerated the contradictions of Japanese capitalism and sent it slithering out of control into the morass of war, thus bringing to the proud Japanese Empire the tragic fate of total collapse.

This philosophy of life did not of itself have a consistent ideology to support it. What gave it its ideological backing was, of course, familism. Its starting point was the ethic of filial piety which spoke of the abundant goodness of our parents, "deeper than the ocean, greater than the mountains," and enjoined absolute obedience. To suppress one's own individuality and behave always in accordance with the welfare of the *ie*, to obey always the order of the household, and to do one's best to get on in the world in order to requite one's duty to one's parents—these were the core elements of a personal ethic for the Japanese. These virtues magnified on a national scale in the family state constituted loyalty—the obedience of the dutiful subject to the Great Imperial Will, the determination to repay the Imperial Blessings with the most sincere reverence for the emperor and the most sincere patriotism. Loyalty and filial piety were linked in a single thread. It was not an ideology which was translated directly into the reality of social life, but it was of sufficient strength to influence the way people really acted. The ideology of the Confucian family system deviated from the real situation in most families, but it did serve to strengthen certain features of that reality. The process of ideological indoctrination which likened the ruler-subject relation to the father-son relation was able to build on general sentiments of national patriotism, direct extensions of more local patriotisms, to give some real relief from their sense of inferiority to the nameless masses.

47

CHAPTER 6

THE STRUCTURE OF FAMILISTIC SOCIETY

When, with the development of society's productive potential, circumstances permit men abundant opportunities
for economic independence, they are able to become free,
independent, and self-reliant actors. Their social relations
are relations of equality based on a mutual recognition of
each other's basic equality as individuals. Even relations of
control and subordination, when they arise, are relations
limited to particular spheres which do not involve subordination of the whole personality. Such are the social relations characteristic of modern society.

However, the modern society which developed in prewar
Japan was not characterized by such relations of freedom and equality. For a Japanese, brought up in a familistic atmosphere, the world beyond the family was a turbulent world, an *ukiyo*, as it was described in a word which
was sometimes written with characters meaning "world of
suffering," sometimes with characters meaning "the floating world." The only way to achieve security in that *ukiyo*
was to forge relationships outside the family which were
also of a *familistic* kind. The parent-child relationship,
which was the axial relationship within the family itself,
was strongly colored with accents of subordination, and it
was this which caused such relationships to proliferate in

Japanese society as a whole. It was by dependence on *oya-bun-kobun* relations which fictively re-created family relationships that one was enabled to survive the vicissitudes of the *ukiyo*. One found someone more powerful than oneself whom one could treat, and address, as *oyabun*—"player of the father role," literally—and who would treat one as his *kobun*—"player of the child role." This feudal familism, as one may justly call it since these relations merged family status with master-servant status, continued to characterize Japanese society even in the modern period: familistic social relations persisted. It was because this was such a striking characteristic of Japanese society that in the immediate postwar period books which analyzed the familistic structure of Japanese society attracted so much attention (Kawashima, 1948), and why, in later years, discussion of the "vertical society" came so much into vogue (Nakane, 1967).

Nowhere were such relationships so typically apparent as in the villages. The landlord-tenant relationships so important for agriculture retained elements of the *oyabun-kobun* connection. The web of dependency, spun around an axis of kinship or its fictive alternatives, was intensified by the daily accumulation of neighborly contacts so that the whole hamlet acquired something of an extended-family character. The penetration of the capitalist economy did something to erode these characteristics, but the familistic nature of social relations remained, albeit in a somewhat attenuated form.

One can clearly see the same phenomenon in the world of the small shopkeeper and artisan. Some older practices, such as the establishment of branch shops symbolized in the "division of the *noren* shop sign," gradually disappeared after the Meiji Restoration, but the employment relations of the commercial world, the status relations between master and errand boy (*detchi*), master and assistant (*tedai*), and

50

master and manager (*bantō*), were long maintained (Nakano, 1964). And, of course, in the small craft workshop much of the old master-journeyman-apprentice relationships remained: the factory owner was the head of something like a factory family. It was the maintenance of these familistic relationships which enabled the tiny craft enterprise to survive in spite of the development of the large factories of modern enterprises. I have already described how the areas of the cities in which such small family enterprises predominated had something of a village character: neighbor relations in these downtown areas were also familistic in character.

By contrast, the relations in which the workers in the modern large enterprises were involved would seem at first sight to be of a different kind. However, the large *zaibatsu* concerns which ran these large factories were themselves, irrespective of their size, *dōzoku* structures of a familistic kind (Fukushima, 1967), and within the separate workshops of these factories social relations were not decisively different from those in the small family enterprises. At first the workers employed were often of the *shokunin* craftsman type who had experience in the smaller factories, though later the large enterprises sought to develop their own core of loyal workers trained by themselves and employed under a system which emphasized seniority status. They sought to build up a family atmosphere in each workshop, and at the same time to create a consciousness of the whole enterprise as one large family. They did so—in their mines, for instance—by policies of benevolent paternalism, welfare facilities, bonuses, etc. (Matsushima, 1951). The holistic slogans of enterprise familism, stressing the unitory bond between employer and employee, became particularly prominent during the war thanks to the organization created out of the earlier trade unions—the

Movement for Service to the Nation through Industry. But in the large enterprises the reality corresponding to those slogans had already been prepared.

Bureaucracy and the world of the politicians also showed the same sort of familistic relationships. Not even the cultural, academic, and artistic organizations, which had the greatest potential for modernity, were exempt. Promotion chances and appointments to official positions were influenced by one's connections with powerful *oyabun*; it was the number of his *kobun* which determined an *oyabun's* authority. The basis for these vertical ties within organizations was often a personal affective one—coming from the same village, having been to the same school, in-law relations, or the relation of a go-between to a young man over whose marriage he had presided. Groups formed on such a basis had a secretive character which was indicated by the term *batsu* used to describe them. A similar familistic, status-hierarchical pattern was found in the organized *yakuza* gangs which controlled gambling and other illegal activities, with their *oyabun-kobun* and (among the followers of a particular gang boss) elder brother-younger brother structure. In bonds which held these groups together—the absolute dominance and protection of the *oyabun,* or "elder brother," and the corresponding subservience and loyalty of the *kobun,* or younger brother—the Japanese style of feudal familism was revealed in its strongest, albeit most caricatured form (Iwai, 1963).

These familistic social relations which penetrated into the furthest corner of Japanese society were essentially adapted to face-to-face primary groups; they were structural principles suitable for "community." But, as we have seen, these all-pervasive principles penetrated associations as well as communities; secondary, functional groups also took on a familistic structure.

In the first place, when functional groups, such as youth

groups or cooperatives, were formed within a geographically defined community, they took on, as was noted above, an all-embracing character: every resident had to belong. The familistic structure of the local community was imported into the functional group and distorted its functional character; instead of being organizations which could be joined by anyone who supported their purposes, they became inclusive organizations involving even those who had no interest in their ostensible purposes. Leadership in such groups, instead of falling as it should to those judged suitable for carrying out the organization's purposes, was assigned to those who already occupied positions of patriarchal leadership in the local community. Such organizations could hardly be expected to be vigorously active, nor was it easy to secure efficient management. But that did not mean that when somebody with suitable qualities did assume the leadership—somebody who was not a traditional patriarchal leader—efficiency was increased. The contrary was often true; familistic man tends to react against rational leadership.

When functional groups are created outside the framework of a local society, however, the leader-follower pattern of community relations cannot be directly imported, and there is a greater chance of an escape from familism. But even in such cases the familistic character of the Japanese can penetrate the organization.

For example, if we take the industrial enterprise as one such typical functional organization, even in large enterprises every worker is expected to be devoted to the prosperity of the firm, as if he were a partner in a small family business; the firm is seen as a kind of *ie* to which one devotes one's whole life. Within this enterprise-as-enlarged-*ie*, the clerical and technical workers had the superior status of *shain,* and the manual workers in the production shops *kōin*. And among the *kōin* there were the status gradations of

53

foreman and ordinary worker, while the whole enterprise was structured as a congeries of workshops, each a small *ie* within which familistic relations prevailed. The father figure was shop superintendent, and the ethic not only required all his underlings to work together as one, but also made it natural that he should take a benevolent interest in their private lives and that they should be prepared to offer him their services if necessary outside of the factory. Management by familistic groupism was the Japanese style.

Where social groups have this kind of familistic structure, their leaders, in much the same way as the househead represented and embodied the *ie,* come easily to think of the group as theirs; the group, and the leader as an individual, tend to become identified. The English word "public" means: "pertaining to the people as a whole, the community as a whole." By contrast the Japanese word *ōyake,* which is used as a translation of "public," derives etymologically from a word meaning "the great house," and once meant "pertaining to the Imperial family." As Aruga (1967) has pointed out, the word *watakushi,* which in modern Japanese translates the English "private" (as opposed to "public"), as well as meaning "I," the first person singular, originally meant a subordinate of an *ōyake* master who was, in his turn, also *ōyake* vis-à-vis his own subordinates. So in the Japanese style the public interest is the furthering of the *oyabun's* interest, and though much is made of the need to "separate the public and the private," in practice they are inextricably intermixed. Just as in the small business the firm and the boss were one, so in the large enterprise too, the distinction between the firm's business and private business was not entirely clear, and the intermingling of the public and private tended to reinforce familistic cohesion by letting everyone gain material private benefits according to his status.

Finally we have to ask what happens to the relationships

between groups, when the groups themselves have this familistic structure and their members are thoroughly immersed
in it under a patriarchal authoritarian style of leadership
which acknowledges no boundary between public and
private.

The first thing to note is that as social groups become
functionally differentiated with modernization, people
begin to develop multiple membership in different groups.
Hence conflicts of loyalty arise, and people may come to
suffer from split personalities. To avoid this, Japanese had
a tendency to concentrate their loyalties on the most familistic groups which offered total support and to keep their
association with functional groups to the limits of the necessary. For example, when workers who owe loyalty to
their workplace form recreational groups, instead of seeking people of similar interests wherever they may be found,
they are likely to make up a group from within the firm.
Group memberships are concentrated within a key group.

Secondly, as the size of modern functionally differentiated organizations grows, and as they necessarily develop a
bureaucratic structure as they become internally functionally differentiated, this bureaucratization takes a special
form when the organization is made up of premodern familistic men. All too easily the division of labor can lead to
factional rivalry; specialization can dysfunctionally give
rise to jurisdictional disputes. Subgroups separated out
within the organization take on a closed familistic character
whence arises a strong sense of "group egoism." However,
such dysfunctional consequences can be avoided when control from the top is effectively exercised through familistic
ties between the head of the whole organization and the
heads of the various subgroups. Then jurisdictional disputes
can be turned into mutual competition in the pursuit of the
goals of the organization as a whole. Where, however, there
is no clear hierarchy of groups, no obvious ranking, then

sectionalism and group egoism can run rampant. Within one's own group one is always under the eye of the chief, and one behaves loyally to the group, but is entitled to behave differently when outside this small in-group. Indeed, the my-group-first principle can make it an act of loyalty to behave in an out-group context in a way that would never be permitted within one's own group. One can be justified in trying to get a member of an opposing faction into trouble because the moral standards for in-group behavior and out-group behavior are different; a difference Max Weber described as that between *Binnenmoral* and *Aussenmoral*.

One way of putting it is to say that the Japanese were obedient to a very vertical family morality in the local community and workplace where they spent most of their lives, but were unable to develop a horizontal morality suitable for the wider world outside. Close to home in their village and neighborhood and workplace, they accepted all the obligations of the relations in which they were involved and feared ever to lose their reputation for honoring them. But once outside that context, those same men and women were quite happy to be, in the words of the proverb, "the traveller who leaves his shame behind him." It is a sad irony that one of the much-quoted phrases of the Imperial Rescript on Education, which was memorized by every schoolchild between 1891 and 1945, should have been in the official translation, "extend your benevolence to all."

CHAPTER 7

THE STRATIFICATION SYSTEM OF PREWAR JAPAN

The familistic groups which we have described in the previous chapter, for all their group egoism, were nevertheless linked together through the network of a capitalist society and organically integrated into the structure of a centralized modern state. Japan was no longer, as it had been in the premodern period, a mere aggregate of discrete isolated and scattered microcosms. It was, indeed, a very powerfully integrated Imperial state. That integration, however, was not the autonomous cohesion of the modern citizen; it was cohesion around the vertical ties of a familistic state, lacking in the bonds of collateral unity. The overall structure of Japanese society was not democratic.

The immaturity of democracy will be apparent from what has been said hitherto, but what part did the stratification system play in the explanation of this immaturity?

The class structure changed, of course, over time. I have not the space for detailed explanation but instead will concentrate on the period of the 1920s and 1930s—the period of the maturing of capitalist society—with a few backward glances at developments since the Meiji Restoration. Table 5 gives some indications, assigning 2.5 percent of the population to the ruling class, 30 percent to intermediate strata, and 70 percent to the dominated class. However, many of

Table 5 The Class Structure of Prewar Japan (percent)

	1909	1920	1930
I Ruling Class	2.3	2.5	2.5
Imperial family, aristocracy, and Imperially appointed officials	0.2	0.2	0.2
Landlords (more than 5 hectares)	0.9	0.8	0.6
Capitalists (more than 100,000 yen capital and 5 employees)	1.1	1.4	1.5
Pensioners (Imperially appointed officials)	0.1	0.1	0.2
II Intermediate Strata	36.3	30.4	29.0
Lower officials	0.5	0.7	0.6
Farmers (owner-cultivators with less than 5 hectares)	22.7	17.3	15.6
Fishermen (paying business tax)	2.5	2.4	2.4
Artisans & retailers (paying business taxes)	6.8	5.9	6.5
Independent professional and technical workers (doctors, teachers, technicians, priests, and free professions)	3.5	3.7	3.4
Pensioners (lower officials)	0.3	0.4	0.5
III Dominated Class	61.4	67.1	68.5
Poor farmers (tenants and part-tenants)	39.5	34.9	29.4
Self-employed workers (exempt from business tax)	7.7	8.4	3.4
Manual workers	13.4	21.4	32.7
Public employees (non-tenured)	0.8	2.4	3.0

Source: Ōhashi, 1971, pp. 26–27. The original table gives only households for farmers and self-employed. They have been recalculated on the assumption that there were 2.5 workers per owner-cultivator household, and 2 workers per other household.

those counted as landlords or capitalists could better be seen as belonging to the intermediate class, and many of the farmers and fishermen in the intermediate class ought properly to belong to the dominated group, thus making the latter larger. Bearing these finer distinctions in mind, I would like here, at the risk of oversimplifying the analysis, to talk in terms of three main categories—the upper ruling class with the capitalists at its core and the large landlords, politicians, and higher civil servants as their allies; the intermediate class, divided into the old middle class made up of small businessmen and retailers and factory owners as well as small landlords; and the new middle class of officials and teachers and white-collar workers in the large enterprises; and the lower, dominated class of farmers, petty traders, self-employed workers, and manual employees.

To begin with the capitalists who made up the core of the upper class, they predominantly descended from the commercial money-lending merchants of the towns of the Tokugawa period. Table 6 shows the results of a study of 200 leaders of the business world in the 1880s. Nearly 80 percent of them were of commoner (*heimin*) status, and more than half townsmen. As many as 20 percent were born into the large merchant houses, including some which developed into the big *zaibatsu* concerns. Former members of the peasantry make up more than 20 percent, but most of them were either country samurai or local rural magnates (Mannari, 1965). The vigorous entrepreneurial activity of these men was, of course, very different from the traditional commercial activity of the old society, but still they were

Table 6 Former Feudal Status of the Elite (percent)

Father's feudal status	Businessmen		Politicians	
	1880	1920	1880	1920
Court aristocrat, feudal lord	0	0	12	4
Samurai	23	37	79	46
higher ranking	1	8	7	3
middle ranking	10	2	23	11
lower ranking	8	8	38	18
Peasant	22	21	6	38
country samurai (*gōshi*)	3	2	4	7
headman, village elder	14	17	1	26
Townsman (*chōnin*)	55	42	3	12

Source: Mannari, 1965, pp. 53, 84.

59

unable to escape from the culture of that society. It is not surprising that the extended-family *dōzoku* system of the old Edo townsmen was kept alive even in the great *zaibatsu* enterprises.

Of contrasting origins were the political leaders of the period, 90 percent of whom were samurai, broadly defined to include feudal lords and Kyoto court nobles: 40 percent of them were low-ranking samurai. Even these members of the political elite, for all the radical antagonism they showed against feudalism, still did not entirely cut themselves off from the spirit of the feudal society into which they had been born. It was through the intimate collaboration of such a political elite that the business leaders managed the process of capital accumulation through purchasing cheaply property sold off by the government and getting government contracts.

The picture changes, however, when we come to the 1920s. The samurai now provide nearly 40 percent of the business leaders and no longer quite half of the leading politicians. About a third of these politicians are from wealthier farmers, chiefly landlords, but even at this stage, the contribution to either set of elites of the lower peasantry, petty shopkeepers, and self-employed craftsmen—who made up the bulk of the total population—remained extremely small. And it is worth noting that the new elite of the 1920s was clearly a highly educated elite. Although university graduates made up only 0.3 percent of the total leaving school even in 1920, with the graduates of specialist high schools adding another 1.8 percent, over 80 percent of the political leaders and 60 percent of business leaders were university graduates.

Higher education had thus become an important condition for membership in the ruling political and business elites, but higher education was by and large available only to the children of the upper strata of the old society. Thus even in the second generation after the Restoration the character of the first generation was reproduced. In the Meiji structure characterized by close association between business and politics, the business elite which constituted the core of the upper class had little to do with liberalism of the night-watchman-state variety. Judged by the criteria of Adam Smith, who never knew of "much good done by those who affected to trade for the public good," Japanese businessmen were charlatans rationalizing their profit-seeking as being "for the sake of the nation."

It is perhaps not much of an exaggeration to say that Japanese politics created its own tradition intimately linked to this charlatanry, one based on the exchange of political contributions and corrupt favors. The senior bureaucrats, for their part, were also largely drawn from the upper strata, since higher education was a prerequisite for office, and through these close connections between business and politics were able to move ("descend from heaven," as the phrase has it) into senior positions in the business world, or to enter the political elite. The monolithic unity of political and business groups was sustained throughout the prewar period, and, it is hardly necessary to add, the halo of the emperor standing at the pinnacle of the system served to reinforce their controlling power.

Next, the core of the middle stratum of prewar Japan was the old middle class which Japanese capitalism largely preserved and used as the springboard for its advance. Many of the small and medium enterprises continued to exist in those sectors which the large enterprises did not penetrate, and in other sectors they developed subcontracting relationships with large enterprises. The dual structure of the Japanese economy was sustained by this middle stratum at the cost of considerable hardship. As already mentioned, the proprietors of the small back-street workshops ran their factories as family businesses, their familistic

61

paternalism—the sharing of joys and sorrows—obscuring the low wages paid their artisan-like workers. The heads of the merchant houses, if the old practice of "dividing the *noren* shop sign" was no longer fully institutionalized, could, still hold out the prospect of their helping their shop assistants to set up independently after long years of service, to secure from them many years of devoted low-paid labor. As long as the surplus population continuously reproduced in the rural areas was constantly seeking opportunities for employment outside agriculture, these familistic labor practices retained their viability.

And in the villages high rates of land rent guaranteed the life-style of the small and medium landlords. Though the number owning as much as 5 hectares of leased-out land did not exceed 100,000, if one adds the smaller landlords with between 1 and 5 hectares of land leased to tenants their numbers exceeded 380,000. And cultivating landlords alone—those who farmed their own land as well as leasing some to tenants—numbered more than 160,000. Given that the owners of large tracts of land usually placed managers in villages where they had tenants and that these managers played a landlordlike role, and given that the total number of Japanese rural settlements was of the order of 135,000, one can assume that in the majority of villages there was a landlord who would qualify for membership in the middle stratum. Their tenants were in the weak position of tenants-at-will whose tenancy could be terminated at the landlords' convenience, and when the harvest was bad they could only appeal to the landlord's benevolence for a reduction in their rent. Not surprisingly, they were deferential: they could not "look the landlord in the eye." The landlords were the *oyakata,* the masters, the petty ruling class of village society. Their importance in Japanese society as a whole diminished with the progress of industrialization, but throughout the prewar period while the agricultural population remained a majority, they never lost their role as pillars of support for the established social order.

These middle strata did not, of course, share identical interests with the ruling stratum. They, too, as owners of the means of production, had something to lose, and as such had something in common with the upper ruling stratum. On the other hand, as Japanese capitalism developed they suffered from the backwash, and, apart from a minority who made good, they were threatened with inevitable decline; to that extent they were not without resentment toward the ruling strata. But still, to preserve their social position vis-à-vis the lower strata they joined hands with the ruling groups. Their base was crumbling, but for that very reason they were conservative, seeking to preserve the existing order. In their villages and town neighborhoods and in the myriad workshops, it was they who were the masters in direct control of the mass majority with whom they maintained familistic social ties. Hence, in the larger society which the ruling strata controlled, these members of the old middle strata served as nodal points in the system to integrate the micro-communities and the workshops into a whole. They were, as it were, the noncommissioned officers of Japanese society, themselves subordinated to the ruling officer class but in command of their own groups and subgroups.

The newer middle strata were weaker than the old. They were fewer in number and they did not, unlike the older middle class, have direct control over a retinue of subordinates. For all their modern disguise, symbolized in the term "white collar," they were in origin mostly from the older middle strata and had the same social character bred into them by their upbringing. They were, moreover, trained within the Japanese structures of the bureaucracy and the large enterprises and served a mediating function between the ruling groups and the old middle strata. It

63

was the bureaucrats of the new middle class who brought the *yūryokusha,* the "men of influence," of the villages and town neighborhoods into touch with state power, and it was the salaried company employees who served as a link between the large enterprises and the small and medium businesses which subcontracted for them. As for what might be called the intellectuals, the journalists and free professionals, sometimes seen as deviant members of the middle strata, they were able in the earlier part of the prewar period to become absorbed as a wing of the ruling echelons. Progressively, however, as the means of social ascent narrowed, they became mere spectators, thrust aside from the mainstream structure of Japanese society. The ideological abstractions of their ideas did not match their actual practice; indeed the constraints of the Imperial state were too strong for such a matching to be possible. They were swept along in the tide of events, and even when they tried to some extent to stem that tide were powerless to do so.

Finally, the vast majority of the populace who made up the lower stratum, locked into the direct control of the older middle strata, were for the most part of rural orgin, the majority of them still farmers. Rural society was the basic breeding ground of communitarian familistic interpersonal relations, but the farmers, even the tenants, were still to some degree propertied, owning some of their means of production and managing their own enterprises. And in their so-called dual nature it was the conservative streak which always overwhelmed emergent leanings to progressive action. Such leanings were apparent in the tenancy disputes of the 1920s, but these were eventually nipped in the bud as the nation moved onto a war footing. As for the workers, for the most part with fathers and grandfathers in the villages, neither in large nor small enterprises did they develop into a modern class-conscious proletariat. Nor was there any modernization of consciousness among the employees in commerce or among petty retailers and artisans. The lower stratum who made up the mass of the people remained divided and segmentalized in their localities and groups, with few mutual ties between them. And in those scattered groups they accepted members of the old middle class as their masters and their *oyabun*. They themselves were the infantry. Their sense of inferiority toward the NCOs—the officers were a class apart—was made tolerable by the fine distinctions among themselves—master infantryman, first class infantryman, second class infantryman; and, to continue the analogy, by their sense of superiority toward the mere supply soldiers of the ordnance corps. And even the supply soldier at the bottom of the ruler-subject, master-servant hierarchy, the hierarchy defined by the principle of *duty,* could take comfort from the other father-son principle of *feeling*: everyone was equally a child of His Imperial Majesty; everyone was a member of the Imperial nation.

CHAPTER 8

MECHANISMS OF THE TOTAL STRUCTURE

We have described the stratification system of prewar Japanese society as a whole. Most of the pyramid was occupied by the subordinated masses which, led by their *oyabun*, the members of the middle strata in their various localities and workshops, formed a broad base which could be manipulated by the ruling upper stratum which stood at the pinnacle of the system.

The will of the ruling class was transmitted through the mediation of the men of the middle stratum who were, at least compared with the subordinated masses, educated men. The messages which came down through the newspapers and the other media were absorbed by the middle stratum and explained by them to their underlings who were too busy making a living to read newspapers. There may have been some distortion in this transmission process, but by and large the wishes of the rulers were transformed into the voice of the people. The voice of the people was not something that welled up from below: locked into their small groups by vertical ties, they lacked horizontal links with others in similar life situations in other groups. Hence, any incipient voice from below failed to acquire that collective reinforcement by which it might have forced the attention of the nation's masters.

The mass of the people in the lower stratum were pre-occupied with the struggle for survival: work left them little time to be concerned with, or to have opinions about, the direction their society was taking. They followed the opinions of their masters, of the middle stratum, and thought it safer to do so. Even if they harbored critical doubts about the world they lived in, their dependence on their middle stratum superiors inhibited any action which might express those doubts. To accept the familistic ties in which they were enmeshed, to keep their place and know their station, was their best way of dealing with their problems. They were rarely conscious in any case of any conflict of interest with the upper stratum ruling groups: to have allowed such consciousness to develop would have led to their exclusion from the locality or the workshop to which they belonged. The forces at work in the society at large seemed to them as much beyond their control as the forces of nature; man-made disasters were no different from natural disasters. Authority could be wielded in accordance with the interests of the ruling stratum, but their attitude toward it—toward *o-kami*, literally "those above," as the government was described—was aptly summed up in the proverb: you can never say no to a crying child or to the lord's bailiff. People who had been brought up on the injunction "wrap up in something long" never saw themselves as having any influence on the trends of the times. To have imagined they had would have been to display a susceptibility to dangerous thoughts. Democratic criticism and debate were not a part of their lives: they were not given to the onerous task of trying to think things through. It was more comfortable to accept the political apathy of tradition, simply to obey—as befitted those who were subjects over whom others ruled.

Such was the manner in which Japan's modernization proceeded according to the wishes of its rulers and toward the goal of "enriching the country and strengthening the army." The industrial elite forged connections with the bureaucracy through the political elite, and were able to pursue their private gain in the guise of the public interest, while urging on the employees of their enterprises the need to "suppress self-interest for the larger good." And thus industrialization proceeded. The ideology of *nōhonshugi,* of agrarian fundamentalism, justified any sacrifice on the part of the peasantry. For the workers who flowed to the factories from peasant households, wages were low enough, as Table 7 shows, to attract charges of social dumping, yet the state succeeded in passing even the attendant social welfare costs on to the peasant households which gave the workers birth and took them back in times of sickness or unemployment.

Table 7 International Wage Comparison, 1914 (yen)

	Textile workers	Coal miners
Japan	.46	.95
England	1.36	3.21
United States	2.50	—
Germany	1.50	2.96
France	—	2.50

Source: Ōuchi, 1952, p. 173.

It was the premodern social structure which permitted this, and hence the ruling class sought consciously to reinforce that structure whenever it showed signs of weakening. On these foundations they were able to raise the Great Japanese Empire militarily to the status of a first class power. The imperialist expansion based on this military strength enabled Japan to gain control over backward countries in spite of the pressure on it from the advanced countries, a development greeted with great enthusiasm by the old middle class elements who occupied an analogous position in their own society. It was supported, too, by the mass of the people who found compensation for their sense of personal inferiority in the proud thought that they were citizens of the land of the gods. As they saw the map of empire expand and the advance into the continent begin, they could enjoy the illusion that they, too, somehow shared in a new prosperity (Maruyama, 1956).

Nor must one forget the important role which education played in forming the personality of individuals in such a way that these structural mechanisms could operate. It was not only that Japanese education failed to foster a critical attitude toward the social environment which molded the Japanese people. From the beginning of the century onward there was conscious fear of the development of critical attitudes and active attempts to repress them. Enrollment rates which could put most of the rest of the world to shame had made almost the whole population literate, but this quantitative expansion of training in the three Rs did not give people the eyes to look at their society critically. Basic state schooling was, one might say, schooling for soldiers. Higher education was the education of officers and NCOs. Vocational schools, higher technical schools, and universities, in their graded hierarchy, were the supply system for a status-ranked society. From such an educational process conducted under full pressure from the Imperial state, one could not expect, even from university education, the development of critical political awareness. The university was the supplier of the officer class, and even after the early days when a degree was an assurance of worldly success ("Bachelor of arts he is: I'll grab him for a son-in-law," the popular song used to go), even after job prospects declined, the universities did no more than create a floating stratum of quasi-intellectuals.

One must beware, of course, of suggesting that the overall structure of Japanese society and its sustaining mechanisms remained unchanged throughout the prewar period. There were considerable changes in the seventy years following the Restoration as industrialization proceeded. There were big differences between Japan before the Sino-Japanese War and the Japan in which capitalism had consolidated its position after the two wars with China and Russia, and even more in the post-World War I Japan in which the forces of monopoly capitalism were broadly consolidated.

As the capitalistic economy develops, men cannot remain the same as they were in the feudal period. The change in the basic economic structure dilutes the community character of villages and urban neighborhoods and cannot fail to affect the social structure. However much, after the failure of the popular Rights Movement, an education rooted in the emperor system sought to make a nation of loyal citizens and filial children, there were limits to such an attempt. Their lives cramped and shaped by the cold logic of a monetary economy, men absorbed some of that economic rationality into themselves: the seeds of individualism were sown and could not be stopped from shooting forth. No attempt to preserve the "beautiful customs" of selflessness and neighborly assistance within the constraining bonds of the local community could succeed in preserving the patterns which prevailed at the beginning of the modern period. Labor relations in a modern enterprise could not be contained within the mold of traditional craftsman-journeyman relations. The white collar workers, whose numbers increased particularly after World War I, could not be treated—even if a lot of them were brought up in the old middle class—like the loyal shop assistants in old Edo merchant families with their aprons and their black sashes. The emergence of a mass society corresponding to the monopoly phase of capitalism was inevitable as this stratum matured, and a popular mass culture based on commercial entertainment began to have a wide influence.

Hence, even in prewar Japan, trade unions came to be formed, even if on a small scale; strikes took place and a peasant movement developed. They were evidence of a loosening of familistic social relations and community restraints, and of the weakening of the bonds which tied the old middle class to their subordinates. But these developments did not represent a major tide in the affairs of Japan as a whole, hence they could easily be suppressed by state power. Horizontal ties of class solidarity were not yet strong enough to challenge the vertical ties of a familistic nature. Some people wrote about *minponshugi*—"democentrism," perhaps the word used to translate democratic ideas into a Japanese context. And the 1920s, did come to be called the period of "Taishō democracy." But the intellectual and spiritual basis for these movements was extremely thin: familistic communitarianism, though weakened, was still pervasively strong in Japanese society.

Thus, the contradictions of capitalist society after the world depression were redirected into confrontation between the haves and have-nots among nations, and Japan moved increasingly onto a war footing. The fact that the emperor was formally commander-in-chief of the armed forces and that military affairs were consequently separate from and independent of the civilian authority which controlled other matters of state was used by the army to propel Japan along the path toward war. And when finally the war began, and became prolonged, the moral campaign for national mobilization was further intensified; with heavy-handed use of the mass media, all the stops were pulled out to glorify "the national essence." The moralism of this campaign did not entirely correspond to the real and pervasive, if latent, spirit of selfishness, the new manifestations of capitalist individualism. The local neighborhood associations of urban wards and village hamlets were integrated into the bureaucratic structure as its grass roots organs, and the old middle class was thereby given authoritative backing, as a means of strengthening control through the ten-household neighborhood groups. These measures were effective up to a point, using as they did the mechanisms described earlier, but it was too much to expect the system to perform the impossible feat of bringing rhetoric into conformity with reality. In such an almost fanatical system of authoritarian control people certainly made a consistent show of obedience—making demonstrative displays of loyal joy when their conscription papers arrived, for instance. But underneath, the effort selfishly to defend one's personal livelihood persisted; the conscription papers were wept over at home. So, as the war situation worsened, authoritarian control had to become even more severe and the pressures of ideological exhortation were stepped up.

Nevertheless, in spite of such gaps between rhetoric and reality, right up to the day of defeat these cracks in the Japanese social structure never developed into open fissures. There was no antiwar movement, and only in the last atom-scorched days did a movement to hasten the ending of the war begin. Such was the success of Japanese society in marrying an ancient, premodern, undemocratic structure with modern machine civilization. Socially, it had reached the stage of monopoly capitalism and produced the cultural characteristics of mass society, but still it preserved the premodern character of the workshop and the self-contained local community. The state structure built on this foundation was kept intact, and ideological indoctrination centered around loyalty to the Imperial state was intense enough to prevent any disturbance of the whole social mechanism. Such were the special characteristics of Japanese society, the essence of the Great Japanese Empire.

PART II

CHANGE IN POSTWAR SOCIETY

CHAPTER 9

DEMOCRATIZATION AND ITS LIMITS

The Great Japanese Empire collapsed with the unconditional surrender of August 15, 1945. (More accurately, the notification of surrender and its announcement by the Imperial Rescript were issued on the 14th, although the latter was broadcast on the following day.) After seventy years on the road to modernization, the seventy years since the Meiji Restoration, the country was ready to start afresh out of the ruins of the war, this time as just plain "Japan."

As defeat became certain with the destruction of the nation's cities by bombing, and then, following the dropping of the atom bombs, with the acceptance of the Potsdam Declaration, the emotions which predominated among the Japanese people were very complex. A bewildered sense of emptiness and loss of identity were conjoined with relief at their liberation from the daily fear of death. Above all, in a situation of total privation brought about by a reckless war, there was the struggle to survive, to get enough to eat. These were the circumstances which saw the proclamation of new political principles: respect for basic human rights and freedom of expression—phrases which were dimly remembered from the 1920s period of Taishō democracy. For most of the population the words evoked little in the way of emotional response. Even the most delicate of dishes does not whet the appetite of those to whom it is unfamiliar, but this was the dish which, in the stern circumstances of a foreign occupation, was set before the people, whether they wanted it or not. A wide range of ordinances for the democratization of Japan began to shake the structure of the country.

In the immediate postwar period Japan got off to a paradoxical start in its new career: democracy was taken as the voice of authority. Not as the result of any internally generated change, but while under occupation by an invading army, Japan was instructed by orders from that army's GHQ to adopt a new value system called democracy. Democratization was imposed from above. Postwar Japan became a kind of test bed for democracy. In that experiment the healthy character of American democracy by and large prevailed. For all the many limitations—that these were policies of a military occupation, that they often took the form of direct importation of institutions unsuited to Japan's real circumstances, and that there lay concealed behind them the strategems and devices of international power politics—one can at least grant that the Occupation policies were informed by the conscience of men, who, in the sulfurous fumes of gunfire which had pervaded the world for so long, had come to understand the wickedness of war.

Thus Japan accepted democracy as the overriding imperative, transformed the absolutist system of Imperial rule into a purely symbolic system of Imperial rule, and through revision of the constitution made drastic amendments in the "national entity" which had hitherto been held sacred and inviolable. The feudalistic family system on which the empire had so prided itself was also legally abolished along with the "national entity" in a revision of the Civil Code based on the modern principles of a family system based on the marital relationship. The *ie* lost its legal status, male primacy was abolished, and a family was redefined as something created anew by the joint agreement of a man and a woman. Equality of the sexes was further guaranteed by an extension of the franchise. In the general elections of 1946, women cast their votes alongside men, and women Diet members appeared for the first time.

The *zaibatsu* which had dominated the prewar economy were dissolved by measures to prevent the concentration of monopoly power. The road to freedom was opened to workers and farmers who had for so long sustained the Imperial regime. Workers were able, thanks to the Trade Union Law and Labor Standards Law, to form unions to defend their rights and to improve hours and conditions of work. Even in the prewar period labor unions had not been entirely absent, and there had even been strikes, but they had received no legal protection and could be suppressed any time at the discretion of the governmental and police authority. Now these were recognized and embodied in law as absolute rights of the workers. Tenant farmers who had been exploited by high rent rates were liberated from their binding shackles by the land reform. Already in the 1930s, as the weight of agriculture in the developing capitalist economy diminished, and with it the relative power of the landlords, there had been some initial measures to create and maintain a system of owner-farming, and to control rent rates. And the Japanese government after the war took further initiatives in this direction. It was pressure from the Occupation, however, which made sure that they were thoroughly and vigorously pursued. As a result, owner-farmers, who had made up only about 30 percent of farming families, came to count for over 60 percent, and the proportion of families wholly dependent on leased land fell from nearly 30 to a mere 5 percent.

Academic freedom and freedom of opinion were also guaranteed and with a new school system the nationalistic education which had fostered support for the empire was transformed. Coming after a repressive period in which even the very name of social science was taboo, the establishment of academic freedom was greeted in the universities with immense delight. Freedom of opinion and expression seemed a precious gift which opened up prospects of social transformation. The ethics and civics courses in schools which had been used to instill in children the perverted prewar ideologies of family and state were replaced by social studies courses. This, too, was a great gain, helping to provide the conditions in which children could grow up as democratic citizens.

The postwar reforms also affected the governmental system. The state structure had always been excessively centralized, and under the wartime regime had taken on more of the character of a police state. In the new system, local self-government was given greater importance and the local government bodies which had until then been mere organs of the state were given fairly wide scope for autonomy. The imposition of national uniformity by the central government was checked, and democratic initiatives became possible at the local level, thus bringing a breath of democracy to the provinces.

These democratic reforms were of the sort that one would expect to develop in a modern society, and they held the seeds of a radical transformation of Japan's premodern social structure. They were capable, too, of fundamentally redirecting the traditional value system. However, the Emperor whose personal broadcast had brought the war to an end without a great upheaval—but in whose name the war had been declared in the first place—did not abdicate his position. Although political leaders were punished by the war crimes tribunal, and others were purged from public office, attempts at a fundamental probing of the responsibility for the war were swallowed up in the vagueness of the formula, "the universal repentence of a hundred million people."

Responsibility for the harm inflicted on the countries which had been attacked was never clearly established. It was symbolic of the tendency for evasion that the Occupation army was generally referred to as the "garrison army," and the defeat as the "end of the war." Nor should one overlook the fact that, because the Occupation army ruled not directly but through the Japanese government, some of the reforms which it initiated were thereby distorted.

Thus it was difficult for the "gift" of democracy to be accurately appreciated, given the passive resistance of what remained of the ruling class, and given that the people at large had no ground soil of experience in which to root the new ideas. For Japanese in whom the familistic value system had been bred in the bone, the new value system called democracy was hard to get used to. Quite apart from which, in the economic conditions which prevailed immediately after the war, extreme poverty in any case made it hard to exercise democratic liberties in a wholesome direction.

Hence, it was easy for liberty to become license. The Japanese knew only the ethical principles of convention, reinforced by the ethics courses in schools which stressed "don'ts" rather than "dos." When the prewar value system came to be rejected in principle and thrown overboard, therefore, it was as if the external brakes had been removed. That no internal brakes were developed and that repressed urges should overflow in decadent behavior was not perhaps surprising. The respect for human rights, which is central to democracy, did not turn into a proper individualism, but served only to bring to the surface the selfishness which was always latently there because fostered by the previous regime. The idea of rights was distorted to justify the open pursuit of private profit. The general breakdown of the status stratification system accelerated the process. The dilution of the atmosphere of

81

communitarian "harmony" as the democratic reforms took their effect created a sense of liberation in which the natural desires of human beings sought satisfaction in the wild pursuit of pleasure. The rejection of the old rhetoric which placed all the emphasis on "spirit" prompted a tendency to grab desperately for things material.

It was perhaps understandable and forgivable that the democratization process should take the form of such excesses and distortions, in a world in which inflation was rampant and the food situation desperate, and among a people to whom democratic freedoms had hitherto been wholly alien. The spirit of freedom which burgeoned along with these distortions was something to be fostered. Even if liberty did run to license, the answer was not to narrow freedom, but to create the conditions under which desires could seek proper and satisfactory expression. But, for those Japanese who had been strictly reared in the prewar atmosphere, the unrestrained behavior of the so-called *après-guerre* generation was insupportable. As they of the older generation began to recover a certain confidence after the first run of democratic reforms, the "abuses" of this kind of democracy provided a rallying point for their recovery. The incompatibility of American-style democracy with Japanese traditions was emphasized, and the process of developing an amended Japanese version of democratic ideals was pushed forward. The process was further accelerated as the world situation changed and the cold war between the superpowers developed. It was less in terms of "an experiment in democracy," much more in terms of "an anti-Communist base" that Occupation policy was framed, and as the one glittering image gave way to the other, it is not hard to imagine what encouragement the conservative ruling strata, deeply imbued with old-style Japanese values, received from the change. As the provisions of the purge ordinances were amended and more purgees were allowed to return to public life, these ruling strata were further strengthened. These were men who had been far more concerned about "preserving the national entity" at the time of the surrender than they were about the fate of the nation's people, men who saw the new constitution as an insult forced on Japan by the Occupation army. Thus was created that special situation peculiar to Japan: the spirit of the established democratic peace constitution was to be radically amended by *conservative* forces.

Nevertheless, such were the scars that war had left on the Japanese people after the atom bombs on Hiroshima and Nagasaki and the destruction of the rest of the nation's cities by conventional bombing, that the "peace clause" of the Constitution which renounced war received wide popular support. What started as a Police Reserve at the time of the Korean War and then became a Security Force and now the Self-Defense Forces was gradually developed as an army that was not an army, but it became an accepted national understanding that it really was strictly for defense. That defense expenditure should be cut to the minimum to concentrate on economic recovery became a central axis of policy during that recovery period and a matter of national consensus. The slogan "enrich the country, strengthen the army," which had summed up the nation's objectives at the time of the first opening of Japan by Perry's Black Ships, was amended. The second opening of Japan by the American Occupation struck out the second half of the slogan. The first half, "enriching the country," became even more centrally important.

The Korean War, which broke out just as the economic confusion which followed the war had begun to settle down into some kind of order, gave the economy its first impetus from mere recovery toward further growth. The government's Economic White Paper of 1955 declared that "the postwar period is over" and pointed the way in which the economy should surge ahead. In a true sense the postwar period was not over, but the economic surge, progress toward "enriching the country," can be dated from this time.

CHAPTER 10

INDUSTRIALIZATION WITH HIGH GROWTH RATES

The proportion of the population in agriculture fell to less than half the total in 1930 and was close to 40 percent by 1940. Primary industries as a whole, including forestry and fishing, absorbed 44 percent of the employed population in that year. Japan had become an industrial rather than an agricultural nation. That proportion rose in the postwar period, thanks to the wartime destruction of industry, to over half the population again, with agriculture employing more than 45 percent. But, as the economy moved from recovery to growth, the agricultural population soon began to fall below its prewar minimum of 40 percent. The fall gradually accelerated year by year until in the 1985 census agriculture occupied only 8 percent, and all the primary industries under 10 percent of the working population.

This amounted to the most rapid decline in the agricultural population that the world had ever seen. Soon after the war there had been 18 million people in the farm population, their numbers swollen by wartime evacuees and refugees from the bombing and from the colonies. This was 4 million more than the approximately 14 million mark around which the agricultural population had been stabilized from the Meiji Restoration until the end of the war. Rapidly declining with industrial growth, the population engaged in agriculture was around 10 million by 1970, of whom the number of main as opposed to subsidiary workers was about 7 million, about half of what it had been twenty years before. Fifteen years later in 1985 the figures were 4.85 million and 3.70 million respectively.

This decline in absolute numbers meant an even faster decline in the proportion of the population engaged in agriculture because the total employed population was going up at the same time. In the 1960s, for instance, the employed population increased by 5 million in the space of six or seven years while the agricultural population fell by 4 million—resulting in a drop in the proportion from 30 to 20 percent; it now stands at under 10 percent. Table 8 is eloquent evidence of the rapidity of Japan's postwar industrialization, the proportion engaged in primary industry falling in a quarter century from 40 to less than 10 percent. The complementary change which accompanied this decline in the primary industry population was an increase in employment in the secondary industries to one-third of the total, and in the tertiary industries which had less than a 30 percent share in 1950 to almost 60 percent. It was manufacturing which grew fastest in the process of high growth, but next came construction, wholesaling and

Table 8   Employed Population by Industry (percent)

	1955	1965	1975	1985
Primary industry	41.0	24.7	13.8	9.3
Agriculture	38.0	22.8	12.6	8.3
Secondary industry	23.4	32.3	34.1	33.0
Construction	4.5	7.1	8.9	9.1
Manufacturing	17.6	24.5	24.9	23.7
Tertiary industry	35.5	43.0	51.8	57.5
Commerce, wholesale & retail	13.9	17.8	21.4	33.1
Service industries	11.3	13.0	16.5	20.5

Source: National Census.

retailing, and the service industries. The industry distribution of population shown in Table 8, with more engaged in the tertiary than in the secondary industries and a very low primary industry population, is already that of the advanced countries of North America and Europe.

We should also take note that the sectors which have grown, the secondary and tertiary sectors, are different in character from what they were before the war. In prewar Japan, textiles predominated in manufacturing, but their share has been drastically reduced. The metal industries, machinery, and chemicals had by 1935 come to employ 35 percent of the manufacturing labor force—less than textiles' 40 percent—but by 1955 their share was close to 40 percent and today is more than half. In terms of output value, the machine-producing industries doubled between 1960 and 1965 and then tripled between 1965 and 1970, growing six-fold over a decade. Steel output increased by 4.2 times in those ten years, and output of the chemical industries 3.6 times. Although textiles and food and drink also doubled in the same period, there is no doubt that the emphasis shifted, during this period of accelerated growth, to heavy and chemical industries. Since 1970, too, growth of around 30 percent in steel and chemicals has been matched by an absolute decline in the textile industries. These industries, once the main axis of Japan's industrialization, have fallen in terms of output value to 5 percent of the total. The postwar drive to develop the heavy and chemical industries has resulted in a shift in the industrial structure: they now account for over 60 percent of total output, with heavy industry alone, thanks to the spectacular advance of the machinery industries, accounting for about 50 percent. In employment terms those machinery industries alone now account for 35 percent of the manufacturing labor force compared with around 15 percent before the war. Rapid growth and investment, the importation of new

technology, and the surging demand for household consumer appliances and motor cars account for this remarkable expansion, which led also—in the heavy industries
generally—to a particularly rapid growth of large-scale
firms, many of which rank as world leaders in terms of size.

The tertiary industries which grew to a much larger size
than the secondary were also different in character from
what they had been. It is a normal feature of the industrialization process that when the growth of the secondary
industry population reaches a certain level it begins to slow
down and to fall in terms of proportion, while the number
of workers in the tertiary industries continues to increase
in both absolute numbers and in proportion. Whereas technological developments make it possible in the secondary
industries for output to continue to increase without much
if any increase in the number of workers, labor-saving technologies are less readily available in the tertiary industries,
and the distribution of a growing output of goods requires
an increasing number of workers. But, as industrialization
proceeds to a higher level, although labor saving may not
be as easy as in manufacturing, certain branches of the tertiary industries also see the development of large enterprises
and notable advances in technology are made. The large-
scale importation of computer technology into finance and
insurance in recent years is an example of this and is something likely to be observed in other parts of the tertiary
sector. In the commercial field, too, with the advent of the
age of mass production and mass consumption, the role of
the large enterprise in the wholesaling, department store,
and supermarket sector is rapidly growing.

These developments, bringing the labor force from the
primary to the secondary and tertiary industries, led to a
marked rise in the proportion of the working population
who were employees. That proportion, which by 1955 had
exceeded the prewar 40 percent level, rose, Table 9 shows,

88

Table 9   Employed Population by Status of Worker (percent)

	1955	1965	1975	1985
Employee	45.8	60.8	69.8	74.6
Self-employed	23.9	19.9	17.4	15.8
Unpaid family workers	30.3	19.3	12.7	9.6

Source: Labor Force Survey.

to 60 percent ten years later and after another twenty years to 75 percent in 1985. Agriculture and fisheries were, of course, largely carried on by independent workers and their unpaid family help, but in Japan a large proportion of commercial business was also concentrated in tiny enterprises of independent and family workers. It is for this reason that the 75 percent share of employees is still somewhat less than the 80 percent or 90 percent of the advanced countries. Table 8 showed that the proportion of the working population in commerce and services is quite large, and it is the predominance of family enterprises without paid employees in this sector which accounts for the difference. It is a difference which still has considerable importance for the understanding of contemporary Japanese society.

Nevertheless the increase in employees in thirty-five years from 1950 from 40 to 75 percent and the accompanying diminution of independent workers from one-quarter to about 16 percent and of unpaid family workers from one-third to under 10 percent is a fact of central importance. Even if the employee proportion has not yet reached the level of the advanced countries, this rapid change is an indication of the extent to which the headlong progress of industrialization in the postwar period has rapidly altered the structure of Japanese society.

CHAPTER 11

RAPID CHANGE IN THE AGRARIAN STRUCTURE

The two leading characteristics of the prewar structure of Japanese agriculture were, first, the extremely small size of operational unit, worked largely by hand labor, and, secondly, the fact that about half the arable land was tenanted and agriculture was dominated by the landlord system.

Japan having been for so long an agrarian country, there was little room left for an expansion of the cultivated area in the modern period. And the number of farm families cultivating the land remained relatively stable, at about five and a half million, from the Meiji Restoration right up to the end of the Pacific War. What these two facts imply is that even the fast growth rate of modern Japanese capitalism was not able to do more than absorb into other occupations the surplus younger sons of farming families; it was not fast enough for heads of households or successor eldest sons to be tempted to migrate from the country to any appreciable degree. Consequently, nearly 70 percent of farming families cultivated less than one hectare, and the "one-acre farmers"—roughly to translate the word *gotanbyakushō* which became a synonym for poverty: farmers with less than half a hectare—made up one-third of farm families. Add to this the increase in tenancy since the Meiji

Restoration and the fact that over 40 percent of farm families had to rent at least some, and another 30 percent, all or
nearly all, of their land. Owner-farmers were less than one-
third of the total, and the rest were kept in a state of dependence on their landlords by virtue of high rents and
instability of tenure.

There was consequently little chance, for the great majority of farmers, of mechanizing their operations and
raising the productivity of their labor. They were too
poor for that. What they could and did do, by the sweat
of their brows, was to try to raise the productivity per unit
area by the improvement of crop strains and the increasing
use of fertilizer. The towns, to be sure, had a stratum of
urban poor who were even worse off, but generally the farmers were perceived as the most deeply unfortunate members of society, unable to escape from deprivation however
hard they worked. Japanese agriculture, though the springboard of Japanese capitalism, was excluded from the
growth experience of the capitalist economy.

Table 10   Farm Households by Tenurial Status (percent)

	Owner-farm-er (owned 95% or more)	Owner-farm-er-tenant (owned 50–95%)	Tenant-owner-farm-er (owned 5–50%)	Tenant (owned less than 5%)
1946	32.8	19.8	18.6	28.7
1950	61.9	25.8	6.0	5.1
1960	75.2	18.0	3.6	2.9
1985	85.2	11.1	2.4	0.9

Sources: Statistics of the Ministry of Agriculture and Forestry, and Agriculture and Forestry Census.

The postwar land reform liberated agriculture at least
from the second of its leading characteristics. I have already
mentioned that the power of the landlords began to decline with the development of the capitalist economy and

by the 1920s the power of the urban capitalist was unquestionably stronger. Consequently, when the reconstruction of the postwar economy made the increased production of cheap rice so important, the Japanese government itself planned a land reform. This was made into a more thoroughgoing measure by Occupation army directive, and the long years of landlord dominance were thereby brought to an end, as already described. The reform could not affect the first major characteristic, the tiny size of the average holding, but at least the majority of farm families became owner-farmers.

These new owner-farmers have been responsible for astonishing developments in Japanese agriculture—not only increases in production of rice, which remains the main crop, but also of fruit and livestock. The mechanization of the threshing process had already become fairly widely diffused in the 1930s, but there was very little use of machinery in land preparation. Soon after the war, however, the small-scale two-wheeled tractor-cultivator began to appear, and recently four-wheeled tractors, rice-planting machines, and combine-harvesters have become widely used. Already in the mid-1960s Japan reached the top of the world league table for the horsepower available per acre of cultivated land—a statistic which reflected, in fact, overinvestment, a function of the tiny size of holding singled out earlier as the leading characteristic of Japanese farm households and one from which they still have found no relief. The cost of this mechanization, together with increases in the cost of chemicals for pest control and of fertilizers, provided a brake on farm incomes in spite of increases in yields.

In any case, the steady increases in agricultural output, which continued in the postwar years, were at an annual rate of 3 to 4 percent—well below the annual increases of more than 10 percent in the GNP as a whole. In 1955 agriculture was still producing nearly 20 percent of the national income. The rapid growth of the economy since then very soon reduced that figure to half its former value, and today agriculture's contribution is a mere 3 percent. The productivity gap between agriculture and the other industries has continued to increase.

The consequence has been that farm families have been unable to maintain themselves by agriculture alone, and there has been a large outflow of the agricultural population. In the prewar period, rural overpopulation survived in spite of the way in which migrants were "pushed out" from farm families, but in the high-growth postwar period labor was strongly attracted out of agriculture into other industries: it was a matter of pull rather than push factors which brought the agricultural population down to under one-tenth of the whole.

However, in spite of this rapid diminution of the agricultural population, the actual number of farm households has fallen by only about 20 percent from the prewar level of five and a half million: after taking a long time to get down to the 5 million level it stood at the end of the 1970s at 4.38 million. The picture is clear: males of the younger ages have moved in large numbers to other industries, but their households have not moved out of farming, which has been left to the older generation and to wives. The rapid spread

Table 11   Farm Households by Source of Income (percent)

	1941	1950	1960	1970	1985
Full-time farmers	41.5	50.5	34.3	15.6	14.3
Minor share from non-agricultural occupations	37.3	28.4	33.6	33.7	17.7
Major share from non-agricultural occupations	21.2	21.6	32.1	50.7	68.0

Sources: Agriculture and Forestry Census, and Agricultural Survey.

of mechanization is the counterpart of this reduction in agricultural labor, and the proportion of farm households with multiple incomes has rapidly increased.

In 1950, when the opportunities for employment were very restricted, half of farm households were engaged full time in agriculture, but as Table 11 shows this proportion was reduced to one-third ten years later and is now under 15 percent. Households earning more than half their income from outside agriculture—hardly farming households at all in the proper sense—have steadily risen from about 20 percent to 68 percent. Perhaps the most striking characteristic of contemporary Japanese agriculture is the fact that more than 60 percent of farm households have no single member engaged full-time in farming, and about 90 percent have no male full-time farmer.

The government responded to these developments with the Basic Law of Agriculture of 1961 and the Program for the Improvement of the Agricultural Structure which followed. However, the so-called Structure Policy never really materialized, and all the talk of Japanese agriculture turning the corner proved to be empty. The contradictions of the agricultural industry deepened as years went by. The foolish over-optimism of thinking that it would be possible to alter the agrarian structure with the expenditure of modest sums had a price that had to be paid—by the offer of short-term relief in the form of regular annual increases in the price of rice. But that, too, began to reach a limit as rice came into surplus supply. In 1969, not only was the price held to the previous year's level; there was a beginning, too, of the production adjustment program—subsidies to take land out of cultivation. In the country once known as the "lush reed-plain of jewelled ears" (to quote the *Kojiki*), agriculture, for so long based on the cultivation of rice, had literally reached a turning point. Farmers who had sustained their living standards by steadily increasing rice production within the system of marketing controls and state purchase guarantees found themselves facing a crisis. The rice surplus required switching to other forms of production, but both livestock farming and fruit farming promised nothing but insecurity. As the pressures on Japan to liberalize agricultural imports increase with Japan's growing economic strength, the switch to other forms of production requires becoming competitive with foreign products, and that, with Japan's cost structures and levels, is extremely difficult to achieve. Add to that problem the fact that the surplus in rice is accompanied by an alarming lowering of the home supply ratio for other foods. Self-sufficiency in grain for direct human consumption is 69 percent, but for auimal feed only 2 percent, making an overall level of self-sufficiency in grain of 32 percent. The crisis of agriculture is a crisis also for Japan.

In spite of this crisis situation, living standards in farm households have on the whole risen considerably. Income levels around 1930 were about 70 percent of those of white collar workers for the average farm household, and even 5 percent below the level of the manual workers whose low wages then occasioned constant charges of "social dumping." If put in per capita terms, the gap would be even wider. Household expenditures showed something like half of farm income being spent on food. The postwar period represents a marked contrast. The importance of food production in wartime gave the farmers leverage, and incomes approached those in other sectors, while in the immediate aftermath of the war farm incomes rose above worker incomes. This situation did not last after the economy got back to something like normality, but the development of subsidiary employments in the high-growth period steadily boosted farm incomes until the average exceeded that of worker households.

By 1972, even in per capita terms farm income had ex-

Table 12 Household Expenditure per Household Member: Farm Families by Size of Holding (per capital expenditure of worker families equals 100)

	All farm families	−0.5ha	−1.0	−1.5	−2.0	−2.0
1960	75.8	79.8	72.5	73.4	77.4	87.4
1970	95.3	106.3	93.1	89.7	86.8	90.3
1985	112.2	124.3	113.7	105.2	103.9	98.2

Sources: Ministry of Agriculture and Forestry, Farm Household Economic Survey; Prime Minister's Office, Household Budget Survey.

ceeded the national average for worker households, and the 1985 figures show income per person to be 12 percent higher. Table 12 shows that in terms of household expenditures, too, there was a 12 percent difference. The Engel coefficient for the proportion of income spent on food was also lower— 21, as against 26 in worker households.

Ever since the Basic Law of Agriculture it has been the practice to refer to farm families which were capable of achieving the average income of worker families from its agricultural earnings alone as "viable farming units." Such units at the time of the law amounted to 9 percent of total farm families and toward the end of the 1960s for a short while exceeded 10 percent, but has how dropped to 6 percent. It is, of course, the earnings from other employments which raise the farm family income above urban levels. The total volume of non-agricultural farm income exceeded agricultural farm income for the first time in 1963, and more recently the difference has grown much wider, thanks in part to the restraint on raising the price of rice. From about 1970 agricultural income made up only about one-third of total farm income, in 1975 the figure was 30 percent, and now has fallen below 20 percent. It will be apparent from Table 12 that it is not the farmers with holdings over 2 hectares, those most likely to be full-time agriculturalists, who have the household consumption levels well in excess of those in urban areas, but the owners of tiny holdings who concentrate on some other employment. It is often said and truly said that farming declines while farming families flourish.

CHAPTER 12

RAPID URBANIZATION

The population in the area defined as towns, as already recorded, had approached 40 percent by about 1940. This was a very considerable increase over the 25 percent of the 1930 Census, and is evidence of the rapid increase in the urban population as industrialization accelerated with the approach of total war.

The wholesale destruction wrought by the last years of war reversed this flow into the cities. Urban dwellers returned to the countryside as a result of bombing and evacuation, and they were joined by large numbers returning from the former colonies to swell the rural population. The urban ratio fell below 30 percent. Even in 1950 it was still well below 40 percent. But by 1953, when the process of amalgamating smaller into larger administrative units began, the size of the urban population had recovered to its prewar peak, and thereafter as the economy moved into its high growth phase the cities began a period of rapid expansion.

In the first ten years of that period, up to 1960, urban growth was concentrated on the large urban centers. Tokyo, Osaka, Nagoya, Yokohama, Kyoto, and Kobe—the six large cities—increased in population by 50 percent, and their share of the total population went from 14 to 18 percent. In the five years that followed, only Tokyo, Yokohama, and Nagoya continued to grow, while in the other three cities growth slowed down. In the last decade and a half, Yokohama has been the only exception to a general tendency for growth to be slower in the larger urban centers, and Tokyo and Osaka have even shown a slow decline. The share of the six large cities has in fact fallen from its peak of 19 percent in 1965 to 16 percent ten years later.

However, this does not mean an end of the urbanization process. In the first place, these figures reflect the saturation of the large cities themselves and the shift of population concentration to the areas surrounding them. Excessive densities in the large cities and high land prices have prompted an increasing inflow into the areas from which commuting into the centers is possible. Table 13 shows the continued population expansion in the three main metropolitan areas: the capital-metropolis (Tokyo, Kanagawa, Saitama, Chiba), the mid-Pacific area (Aichi, Gifu, Mie), and the western-central metropolis (Osaka, Hyōgo, Kyoto, Nara). Their 39-percent share in 1960 had grown to 46 percent in 1970 and 48 percent in 1985—about half the total, though the increase since then seems not to have been great.

Table 13   Increasing Population of Three Metropolitan Areas (total pop. = 100)

	1955	1960	1970	1985
Tokyo metropolitan area	17.1	18.9	23.0	25.0
Kyoto/Osaka/Kobe area	12.2	12.9	14.8	14.7
Nagoya metropolitan area	7.6	7.8	8.3	8.5
Total	36.9	39.6	46.1	48.2

Source: National Census.

Table 14 shows what this has meant in terms of the size distribution of cities. As the growth rate of the large centers

100

Table 14 Distribution of Population in Cities of More than 100,000 Inhabitants

| | 1960 | | 1985 | |
	No. of cities	% of total pop.	No. of cities	% of total pop.
1,000,000+	6	17.9	11	20.6
500,000+	3	1.9	10	5.6
300,000+	12	4.6	39	12.3
200,000+	22	5.5	39	8.0
100,000+	71	10.6	104	11.7
Total	114	40.5	203	57.5

Source: National Census.

has slowed down, the growth in smaller cities has increased. Between 1960 and 1965 there was particularly marked growth in cities between 100,000 and 500,000. In the succeeding five years the greatest growth was in cities between 200,000 and 300,000, while in the next five years, from 1970 to 1975, there was a further slowing of growth in the 500,000-and-over categories, and the small cities from 50,000 to 100,000 came to show a rate of growth comparable with the slower-growing cities of 100,000 plus. The effects of urbanization under rapid economic growth had begun to reach the smaller cities.

These figures have, of course, to be seen in the context of administrative measures to increase the number of cities. The amalgamation of administrative areas, begun in 1953, created a number of cities which included wide areas of rural settlement. As a consequence, some administrative cities can no longer be counted as urban areas, nor can the city population be equated with the urban population. When the amalgamations were more or less completed in 1957, there were 501 cities, and in the subsequent thirty years they have grown by 151 to 652. Insofar as these new cities include some rural areas, a certain discounting of changes in the urban population figures as a measure of urban growth is required.

If one takes 100,000 inhabitants as the cut-off point and assumes that administrative units above that size are likely to have a definite urban character, then, as shown in Table 14, the number of such cities increased sharply in the twenty-five years from 1960 to 1985 from 114 to 203 and their share of the total population from 40 to 58 percent—well over half the population. Adding on the 50,000 to 100,000 category, the figure rises to 70 percent.

The typical Japanese city has been a consumer city, once a castle town in the Tokugawa period and later a center of prefectural government. There are exceptions, towns which have become urban centers only since the Meiji period, such as the industrial cities of Yawata, Kawasaki, and Hitachi or the port cities such as Yokohama, Niigata, and Aomori which developed first as ports opened to foreign trade and later acquired prefectural town functions. But for the most part, the pattern has been for consumption cities originally developed as political centers to increase in size as they acquire new industrial functions. The postwar pattern of urban growth has been no different. Formally, postwar Japan is a decentralized state with an emphasis on local self-government, but in effect the central government exercises considerable control over the prefectures and the prefectures over the cities, towns, and villages. This strong centralization of power in practice has been one factor which explains the concentration of population in the capital of Tokyo and, in the provinces, in the prefectural towns. Quite a number of cities have drawn population by virtue of their administrative and political functions, and then had their growth accelerated by a consequent development of industry around them.

However, despite the continuation of this pattern of urban growth, much of the expansion in recent years has come from cities with a relatively heavy concentration in industry. In particular, with the switch from coal to oil energy, there have been towns emerging around heavy industrial complexes with a major chemical plant at their core. Many of the areas newly designated as cities, too, have been genuinely new urban concentrations on the outskirts of the larger metropolitan centers, rather than the result of amalgamating existing towns and villages, the orgin of many new cities in the 1950s. The common pattern is for a small existing town within a metropolitan area simply to swell rapidly in population, to be upgraded from town to city, and to continue to grow in size. The metropolitan areas have thus grown without much increase in the population of the metropolitan cities themselves.

One can summarize the significance of the growth of the urban population as follows. First, as the large cities become too densely populated, the high prices of land caused by the failure to develop a rational land policy place limits on further growth. Secondly, local provincial centers have all increased in size, but the growth has been most spectacular in the industrial cities. Thirdly, along with the continued expansion of the original industrial cities, economic development has also brought a rapid growth of new industrial cities, particularly along the Pacific coastal belt. Since 1963, with the planning of new industrial cities, this growth has spread from the Pacific belt to other areas, including some cities built on green-field sites from the foundations up. Fourthly, and this relates to the first two trends, satellite urbanization around the metropolitan cities is also repeated around the provincial centers—an aspect of urban development particularly marked of late.

Generally speaking, this urbanization has not been a matter of packing more people into existing urban areas which have in some way been redeveloped, but rather the result of cities expanding into what were once rural areas.

Towns are eating into the countryside. The counterpart is the draining of population away from the rural areas remote from the cities, leaving them, in contrast to the high densities of the cities, with problems of low population density. One might say that the growth of cities has made Japanese society in general an urban society. Not only have many rural areas become city areas, but overflowing urban energies have affected the remaining rural areas and brought about a general urbanization of Japanese life— "urbanization" being used here in the sense in which Louis Wirth (1938) used it when he talked of "urbanism as a way of life"—that is to say, something that can pervade a whole society. And it relates closely, of course, to the trends toward mass society.

We have already seen that prewar Japan, in spite of two-thirds of a century of modernization, was still, as a whole, a rural society. Ronald Dore has drawn attention to the contrast between Britain, where the flow of population into the industrial towns after the industrial revolution brought many problems of urban disorganization resulting from the difficulty the new migrants had in adapting to urban life, and Japan where such problems were much less acute. He suggests that one reason might have been the existence of neighborhood and ward associations in Japanese cities, which functioned somewhat like villages and could absorb the immigrants with fewer problems of dislocation (Dore, 1958). The cities, as discussed in Part I, had a rural character. So, even after a fair degree of urbanization as modernization proceeded, the flesh and blood of the society's politics was still rural in character. Households were responsible for their own welfare, and matters the family could not cope with were taken care of by local communitarian associations; there was very little consideration for building the institutions and installations of a social and public character that are necessary in large cities. Prewar

Japan, with its single-minded concentration on rapidly enriching to country and strengthening the army, could devote all its energies to the development of industry and armaments, and gave little thought to the improvement of the living environment or to providing any social forms of welfare security.

Postwar Japan, however, has genuinely become an urban society. If one uses the formulations of Tönnies, who took the metropolis as the extreme form of the *Gesellschaft*, it has become a metropolitan society. The character of the society has changed. In spite of this, however, a pattern of economic growth solely for the purpose of "enriching the country" has slowed down the development of the institutions and installations which this degree of urbanization requires. In the last years of the war, many of Japan's cities were reduced to ashes by bombing, but with a few notable exceptions the reconstruction was rarely properly planned. Piped water systems had become taken for granted in the cities in the prewar period, but the tradition of keeping cesspits in houses and emptying them regularly to take human fertilizer back to the villages had prevented much attention to drainage or to the sort of town planning which in the West sprang naturally from concern with sewer systems. This tradition continued in the postwar period and led to a policy of letting urban expansion run its natural course—i.e., a policy of permitting rampant and unplanned growth of urban areas. The lack of any rational land policy prevented the reservation of areas in the growing towns for environmental facilities, a feature which is all of a piece with the economics-first mentality which lay behind the policy of "enriching the country." The backwardness in imposing controls to protect urban amenities was doubtless one factor in accelerating growth, and that growth has radically transformed Japan, but it has left characteristic problems in its wake, nonetheless.

CHAPTER 13

THE CHANGING STRUCTURE OF EMPLOYMENT

The increase in the proportion of employees in the working population from 40 to 70 percent was an important aspect of social change in postwar Japan, an index of the transformation of Japanese society from one dominated by independent producers to one dominated by employees. Rapid industrialization and economic growth increased the proportion of both white and blue collar workers. As the process of industrialization shifted from simple mechanization to the automation of machine tools and handling devices—as, typically, in the introduction of transfer machines into automobile manufacture—new processes of mechanical automation make real mass production possible and this in turn makes necessary mass sales techniques. Japan's high growth rate made for spectacular and concentrated advances at this stage through the importation of a wide variety of new technologies. In spite of a great deal of labor saving through automation, markets grew even faster both internally and externally, and the number of production workers increased. There was a corresponding increase in white collar workers for general management as enterprises expanded, for personnel management as organizations grew in size and complexity, and for sales as markets became increasingly extended. The transition to the age of mass production and mass consumption also involved a corresponding increase in the number of workers engaged in commerce.

Table 15   Occupational Structure of the Labor Force (Percent)

	1955	1965	1975	1985
Professional and technical workers	4.9	5.6	7.6	10.5
Clerical workers	8.7	13.0	16.7	18.4
Sales workers	10.6	11.7	13.3	13.9
Farming/forestry/fishing workers	40.4	24.5	13.8	9.2
Production workers	24.1	30.1	31.7	31.1

Source: National Census.

These trends are clearly reflected in the figures in Table 15 showing the changing occupational structure of the labor force (though these figures also include independent workers and employers). By 1955 production workers had reached 24 percent of the total, back to the prewar level, but ten years later the figure had grown to 32 percent at the end of the period of high growth; their share fell slightly thereafter and stood at 31 percent in 1985. In spite of the increase in output, rationalization through the adoption of new technology meant that large increases in the labor force were not required. By contrast, the proportion of clerical workers, which was less than 10 percent in 1955, grew steadily thereafter and continued to grow after the reversal of the growth of production workers, to 18 percent in 1985. The growth in the number of sales workers also continued.

In recent years Japan's industrialization has moved on to even higher levels. In production, process automation brings central control systems embodying automatic servo-mechanisms, while business automation—the increasing use of computers for administrative work—has become widespread. The increase in the number of professional and technical workers reflects this upgrading of technological levels.

This development in the stages of industrialization has important implications for the quality of the work experience. The basic character of wage employment in capitalist society consists of the sale of labor in exchange for wages, and in the sense that one is constrained during the hours of work, that labor is forced labor. The craftsman of the feudal period was an independent artisan who owned his own means of production, worked in his own home, and could find meaning in his life through the pleasure of producing goods which he had made himself. In contrast, the modern worker commutes to a factory where he owns none of the means of production and works within a fixed time-constrained division of labor. It is difficult for him to find anything in his work which gives meaning to his life. However, at the stage of simple mechanization the workers' skill remained important; shop-floor groups centered on skilled workers but made up largely of unskilled workers formed identifiable units, and there was always the possibility of satisfaction for the unskilled worker in upgrading himself to skilled status. This was the prewar stage of development, the stage in which independent craft work and pre-automation factory work predominated. But with rapid growth and the transition to higher stages of development, the bulk of production work came to be made up of highly simplified and subdivided tasks. Men were controlled by machines rather than controlling machines themselves. When all that was expected for them was faithfully to fulfill their norms as the work flowed toward them on the conveyor belts, workers were reduced to the status of mere cogs in a work-flow system. The typical worker of the machine age had to be prepared, at least for the hours of labor, to submit to being deprived of his identity.

With the progress of process automation, however, workers are liberated from direct involvement in the production process, and their work increasingly consists chiefly of watching and adjusting meters and instruments. The progress of automation reduces physical labor and increases the proportion of supervisory work requiring a certain degree of technical knowledge. The technological revolution requires workers to have, not so much skill accumulated through years of experience, as a high level of cognitive training. In this way the gap between blue collar and white collar worker narrows as the wages of the former increase. Add to this that the recent development of business automation requires a large number of clerical workers, such as key punchers and word processor operators, to become manipulators of machines. Although there may still be a difference in work environment between factory and office, in iubstance this also reduces the distinction between the nature of blue collar and the nature of white collar work. It is not surprising that the word grey collar has been invented. Here, then, along with the increase in the proportion of employees in the work force, is a second great change—the change in the substantive nature of work—which differentiates contemporary Japanese society from the society of the prewar period.

There is another trend which should not be overlooked, and that is the fact that the increase in employees from 40 to 70 percent of the work force is in part a function of the increase in female employment. In prewar Japan the daughters of poor farm families frequently were sent to work for a period as factory operatives. Factory work for women was generally seen as an exceptional thing occasioned by family poverty: the proper place of women was in the home working as unpaid members of the family labor force. Later, as some occupations such as those of telephone operator and bus conductor were opened to women, these, too, were seen as on the same level as factory work. Even when women with modern ideas entered occupations which required a certain intellectual skill, they were usually referred to as "professional women" and there was a certain derogatory note implied in the term. These prejudices against women's work were somewhat modified by the wartime labor mobilization of women, and in the postwar period when equality of the sexes became a slogan and equal legal rights were assured, the number of women employees steadily increased. Table 16 shows how in the period of rapid growth the proportion of women among employees increased, and the proportion of working women who were employees rather than family workers increased.

Table 16   Women Workers by Occupational Status (percent)

	Employees	Self-employed	Family workers	Total
1955	28.4	19.4	71.2	39.2
	(33.1)	(11.9)	(55.0)	(100.0)
1985	36.1	26.3	81.4	38.8
	(70.5)	(10.3)	(19.3)	(100.0)

Sources: National Census.
Note: The top row in each set of figures shows the proportion of the total category who are women. The second row (the figures in parentheses) shows the distribution of women among those categories.

In spite of a slight decrease with the oil crisis and the temporary halting of growth, the number of women workers has continued to increase since 1976 and by 1985 had reached 36 percent of total employees. Women suffer considerably from the tension between home and work: most tend to work until marriage, when they leave their jobs to become full-time housewives, subsequently taking up jobs again after their children are grown up, a pattern which puts them at a very considerable disadvantage as compared with male workers. This comes out in statistics which show, for example, that women workers have on average seven years' seniority compared with male workers' twelve, and their wages average only 60 percent of male wages. Though they are in this way far from being employed on a footing of equality, nevertheless the great increase in the employment of women must count as one of the significant changes of the postwar period.

To complete the picture of changes in employment, one cannot omit the labor unions. We have already seen that unions did, in fact, exist in the prewar period. But it is only a slight exaggeration to say that they had a negligible significance. Only 410,000 workers were in trade unions in 1935, less than 7 percent of those in wage and salary employment. After the war, however, with the Trade Union Law of 1946, there was a rapid growth of trade unions. Three and three-quarter million had joined trade unions by the end of that year, a unionization of 40 percent. Rapid growth continued as the unions were carried along on the tide of democratization, and in the 1948 and 1949 period the number of union members reached 4.6 million and the unionization rate 56 percent. However, this sudden expansion gave way to a period of consolidation and curtailment, and the unionization rate fell 10 points in 1950. The fall has continued in spite of the steady increase in the number of union members with the growth of the economy. The 5.8 million union members of 1950 have grown to 12.42 million in 1985, but the unionization rate has reached the low level of 29 percent. This is in spite of an increase over those twenty-five years in the number of unions from 40,000 to 74,000 and is partly explained by the fact that a large part of the increase in the labor force has been in manufacturing and the service industries where unionization rates are low. Unions exist in the large enterprises almost without exception, but are often entirely lacking in small firms.

Increased employment in such firms, therefore, is not reflected in an increase in union members. Nor is the union movement itself, with its sectionalized national structure, capable of extending itself into such firms. Again, though, the fact that 30 percent of workers are in unions, when compared with the prewar unionization rate of 7 percent, still counts as an important feature of postwar social change.

At least it is a unionization rate higher than America's 25 percent if low by comparison with Britain's 55 percent or West Germany's 40 percent. Perhaps one should be more concerned about the form the unions take than about their membership coverage: the majority are organized on an enterprise basis, and integrate white collar and blue collar workers in a uniquely Japanese fashion. These enterprise unions echo the so-called enterprise family policies of the management and help to create a situation in which workers can quite happily exhibit a dual loyalty to both firm and union without any sense of contradiction. In this form the familistic social structure of the prewar period lives on in spite of the structural changes in the nature of work, but it must be acknowledged that this very enterprise-based structure of trade unions—clearly a limitation on their effectiveness as trade unions—has at the same time, as we shall see later, been one of the factors which have promoted the high growth rate of the Japanese economy.

CHAPTER 14

THE DEVELOPMENT OF MASS SOCIETY

As the capitalist economy evolved and the proportion of employees grew, an increasing number of people found themselves cut loose from the communitarian neighborhood societies of village and urban ward. For most of them, who had work places to which they travelled daily, their neighborhood was little more than the place where they had their house. Outside of their workplace, these members of the new middle class and workers differ in crucial respects from the family enterprisers of the old middle class; they were simply unit members of an unstructured mass. In their offices and factories, the majority of them are responsible for nothing more than a single simple function within a complex organization, and in their bureaucratized trade union, too, they play a passive manipulated role. Nor does their local neighborhood offer them any opportunity to regain their humanity. Alienated, as they are likely to be, from the pattern of personal relations which prevails in the village and urban neighborhood organizations, which continue to be dominated by the remaining family enterprisers, they have nothing to which to devote the hours when they are liberated from the workplace except mass culture and mass entertainment.

Sociologists refer to this trend as "the development of

mass society." Its beginnings, in Japan, can be seen already in the 1920s when Japanese capitalism began to enter the monopoly stage, and industrialization had reached a fairly advanced level. The trend was fairly clear, that is to say, from the period known as the days of Taishō democracy up to the period of mobilization for war.

But the full development of mass society had to wait until the postwar period of rapid growth—the growth which brought Japan to the stage of advanced industrialism or mass consumption to which the notion of mass society corresponds. We have already mentioned the rapid increase in both white collar and blue collar workers and the narrowing of income differences between them: if not exactly a middle class enjoying a long-term guarantee of secure income, they were at least sufficiently well off to play the role of mass consumers in an advanced industrial society. And they had the leisure to be the carriers of a mass culture, the consumers of mass entertainment. The conditions for mass society were there.

Karl Mannheim first used the phrase "mass society"—*Massengesellschaft*—in his *Man and Society in an Age of Reconstruction,* which he published in Holland in 1935 after he had been driven from Germany two years earlier. The theory of mass society was meant to be a warning. In situations such as gave rise to Nazism, the irrational behavior of the masses can help to establish anti-democratic forces which both manipulate the masses and offer them, in blind obedience to power and authority, an escape from loneliness and anxiety. Since then, the concept has been developed in any number of different directions by a variety of sociologists, and it is now widely used, not just in the context of the collapse of liberal democracy and the rise of totalitarianism, but more generally to describe a society in which a mass of atomized individuals live in unorganized mutual isolation, are subject to feelings of loneliness and

116

anxiety, and lack security and ties of personal intimacy. It is generally assumed that such a society emerges with the breakdown of "citizen society" as the modern, self-regulating functions of communities and associations are weakened. The processes whereby a society, ideally formed by a "public" of rational men and women, can become a diffuse mass society of irrational crowds, easily manipulated by the elite and overgiven to conformity, have been much discussed in America.

What can one say about Japan in these terms? First, perhaps, that men and women cut off from their ties of local neighborhood communities were thrown into the maelstrom of mass society before they had matured into modern members of citizen society. Secondly, though, that there is a strong tendency to find reference groups in, and to conform to the society of, the workplace, as a refuge from the sense of loneliness and helplessness which mass society brings. Alike as all the members of mass society are in being cut off from the ties of neighborhood community, nevertheless they differ, severally, in origins, in occupation, and in social stratum, and they lack any bond which can unite them to their fellows. With no community to protect them from loneliness and helplessness, lacking in common traditions and customs, they live in a state of what Durkheim (1897) called anomie. The bustling crowds of the city form their natural home, and they are part of the anonymous, undifferentiated majority.

Mass societies call for mass communication, and the development of the communications media has also been rapid in the postwar period. Until the 1920s, in the world at large, the printed media of newspapers and magazines, supplemented by silent films, formed the core of the mass media, and in Japan, too, they were joined in 1925 by the beginning of radio broadcasting. But the real developments of mass communications had to wait until after the war.

117

Television broadcasts began in 1953, with color transmissions being added in 1960, and these became the core of the system: the so-called television age had arrived. When transmissions began the Japanese economy was still in the phase of reconstruction; sets were expensive and their ownership was restricted. But the proportion of households owning television sets, which had been a mere 51 percent (all black and white) in 1960, had risen to 94 percent five years later, and today nearly every family has a color television set. Television has become an indispensable part of everyday life and exercises a powerful influence on its viewers. According to Time Budget Studies conducted by the government broadcasting system, NHK, the daily average viewing time is 3 hours and 20 minutes—between an hour and an hour and a half longer than in other industrial countries. Television has brought great changes to the structure of everyday life, and also, it may be added, led to the decline of the cinema which once dominated the culture of visual imagery.

The importance of newspapers, formerly the main means of mass communication, was correspondingly reduced. Nevertheless, even today, the industry is in a healthy state with 565 daily newspapers being printed for every 1000 persons, the highest level in the world. Many newspapers have close connections with television and radio stations and have their own commercial networks, a comprehensive web of mass communication has been created under the control of a small number of capitalist newspaper enterprises which also respond to mass demand with weekly magazines and sports newspapers. Some powerful publishing houses have also entered the weekly magazine field and acquired a supplementary role in the creation of mass culture.

But what function *do* the mass media play in the period of transition to the mass society?

At the beginning of the television age there were critics

who warned that Japan would become a "land of a hundred million idiots." Mass communications, the implication was, may provide large quantities of information, but the masses who receive it are homogenized by its influence; low-level entertainment programs serve to empty the heads of the whole population. The mass communications do create new wants and serve to change premodern value systems: there *are* aspects which it would be a mistake to dismiss simply as the cultivation of mental backwardness. But, at the same time, it is hard to deny that commercial mass communications run to sensationalism when they tend to an excess of low-level entertainment programs that can have undesirable dysfunctional effects for the mass of the people.

The reason why the mass media—primarily television—have these effects may be found in the fact that they depend primarily on advertisements for their operation. For newspapers, the ratio of purchasers' payments to advertising income is of the order of 40:60; they are heavily dependent on advertising. But commercial broadcasting derives 100 percent of its income from sponsors' advertisements.

Table 17 Advertising Expenditure by Medium (percent)

	News-papers	Maga-zines	Radio	Tele-vision	Other
1955	55.3	5.8	16.1	1.5	21.3
1965	35.8	5.6	4.7	32.3	21.6
1975	33.1	5.4	4.9	34.0	22.6
1985	28.7	6.6	5.2	35.2	24.3

Source: Dentsu Incorporated, "Nihon no Kōkokuhi" [Japanese advertising expenditure].

Advertising expenditure has grown by leaps and bounds in the contemporary world of mass production and mass consumption. The distribution between media has changed as shown in Table 17, with the newspapers now receiving below 30 percent compared with the half they received thirty years ago and television's share far exceeding that of newspapers. Television commercials are the more effective in appealing to two senses; they stimulate mass consumption and create fashions. Sponsors, concerned about the effectiveness of their advertising expenditure, emphasize the importance of viewer ratings; hence a tendency for low-level programs that will attract the maximum number of viewers.

This, at least, is an entirely new postwar phenomenon, something which marks a sharp difference from the kind of mass society which began to appear in the 1920s only to be nipped in the bud. It is for this reason that one must count the emergence of a mass society as forming, along with the sharp decline in agriculture, urbanization, and change in the employment structure, a fundamental aspect of postwar social change.

But there have been other marked changes in popular entertainment in the postwar period. Much of everyday entertainment is provided by the television in the home, but the total amount of free time in this so-called leisure age is a good deal greater than before the war, and this has also led to a big increase in pleasure travel and growth in the tourist industry. Equally marked is the growth of gambling as popular entertainment in the form of pachinko pinball saloons, bicycle races, horse races, and speedboat and motorbike races. Pachinko was apparently to be found before the war in entertainment places primarily intended for children, but immediately after the war it rapidly became an adult pastime and still holds its place. The opportunity for a brief escape from reality, suspending time in front of the machine as one's eye follows the tiny spinning balls, while at the same time mildly indulging the gambling instinct—and for the expenditure of very small sums of money—gives pachinko a strong and continuing hold. Bi-cycle races also developed in the postwar period when local authorities began operating public gambling facilities as a source of revenue, and they rapidly spread through the country. Speedboat and motorbike racing were added, also something not seen before the war. Japan is not alone in seeing a spread of gambling in the social circumstances of mass society, but, though one does not wish to be mor-alistic about it, it can hardly be called a healthy phenome-non. Economic growth may have brought a rise in living standards, but daily life is still full enough of anxieties and frustrations to tempt people to gambling forms of enter-tainment as a means of escaping reality and satisfying the risk-taking instinct. This is one aspect in which contem-porary mass society differs from the Japan of the prewar period.

Nor are these public forms of gambling the only means for temporary escape from reality. Among the fans of pro-fessional baseball poring over the sports newspapers, one can see something of the same desire to escape reality and forget one's worries. This is far healthier than gambling, and the growing interest in sports is in itself desirable. But participating in sports is better than merely watching, and the facilities for regularly enjoying sports are limited. Golf courses and swimming pools, which pay their way on a commercial basis, may get built, but there are very few sports grounds available for the casual pleasure of the mass of the people. Nor should one forget the inadequacy of the facilities for continuing education provided by local au-thorities.

As will be discussed later, people have come to give more importance to their free time, and the enjoyment of leisure has become one of the purposes of life. But the original English word "leisure," which we borrow as the word "*rejaa*," in its original sense meant to devote one's free time

121

to "study." When leisure time is actually used for self-cultivation and the development of an interest in society and politics, then and then only can it provide pleasure which rises above the level of momentary enjoyment and gives meaning to human life. It is hard at present to see prospects of such a development.

CHAPTER 15

THE IE SYSTEM: ITS DISSOLUTION AND SURVIVAL

We have already seen how the Japanese family was structured on the lineal principle. Given also that fertility was high, it is not surprising that the average household size before the war was quite large—around five persons. In the reconstruction phase after the war, that average size did not decrease; in fact, for a brief period immediately after the defeat it even showed a slight increase as a result of the postwar baby boom and the worsening of the housing situation which prevented families from dividing. The decrease in household size began as the economy moved from reconstruction to growth. The 1955 figure of 4.97, still at a prewar level, had fallen ten years later to 4.05, and in another twenty years to 3.23, a decrease in three decades of 1.74 persons.

This latest figure for household size is comparable to that found in Europe and North America and explains why people have come to talk of "the emergence of the nuclear family." What that phrase means in terms of the structure of households is shown in Table 19. Along with the rapid increase in single-person households which is also clear from Table 18, there has been a rapid decline in the number of households "including other relatives"—primarily three-generation households—and a steady increase in nuclear families including a marked growth in households consisting of a single married couple. If one counts as nuclear family households those containing a married couple and their unmarried children or a married couple alone, or unmarried children with a single parent, their proportion had reached 63 percent by 1985, having been

Table 18   Distribution of Households by Size (percent)

	1930	1955	1965	1975	1985
1 person	5.5	3.5	8.1	13.5	17.5
2 persons	11.7	10.8	14.3	16.8	19.1
3 persons	14.8	14.5	18.2	20.0	18.7
4 persons	15.1	16.6	22.2	26.5	24.6
5 persons	14.5	16.6	16.1	12.5	11.5
6 persons	12.7	14.1	10.7	6.5	5.4
7 persons	9.9	10.3	6.1	2.8	2.3
8 persons	6.8	6.5	2.5	0.9	0.6
9 and over	9.0	7.1	1.9	0.3	0.1
Average household size	4.98	4.97	4.05	3.45	3.23

Source: National Census.

Table 19   Ordinary Households by Household Type (percent)

	1955	1965	1975	1985
Kin-linked households	96.1	91.8	86.2	82.3
1. Nuclear households	59.6	62.6	63.9	62.5
Married couple only	6.8	9.8	12.4	14.3
Married couple and children	43.1	45.4	45.7	41.6
Father and children	1.6	1.0	0.8	1.0
Mother and children	8.1	6.4	5.0	5.6
2. Other forms of kin-linked households	36.5	29.2	22.3	19.8
Non-kin households	0.5	0.4	0.2	0.2
Single-person households	3.4	7.8	13.5	17.5

Source: National Census.

less than 60 percent twenty years earlier. This may not seem like a very big increase, but if one takes kin-linked households alone the thirty-year period showed an increase from 62 percent to 76 percent. Of course, the spread of nuclear households to over 60 percent of the total does not necessarily mean that all these households are based on the principles of the marital household system. Some, even if they are at the moment nuclear households, may still be operating according to lineal principles and will cease to be nuclear in structure as time passes and a child marries and continues to live with the parents.

Nevertheless, the figures in these two tables do make quite clear that the Japanese family has changed its structure in the postwar period, and it is common to describe this tendency as the "nuclearization" of the family. The term "nuclear family" was established as a technical term by George P. Murdock in his book *Social Structure,* and in 1949, when his book was published, there was no established Japanese translation for the term in use among sociologists. That by now this technical term should have come into common usage in the Japanese language is an indication of the great speed at which structural change is occurring in the Japanese family.

But what do these changes in structure mean in substantive terms?

It is no exaggeration to say that the revision of the Civil Code after the war was a direct challenge to the uniquely Japanese *ie* system and its long traditions. Of course, legal change did not immediately mean a change in reality, and as social custom the *ie* system lives on today. But the change in the legally embodied system of values relating to the family could not fail to have an effect on the reality of family life. The lineal family, with the passage of time, and with the steady decrease in the proportion of family enterprises, has steadily faded as a social form.

One might cite, as the first example of change, the weakening of a sense of "family status." This was particularly strong in rural areas, but even in the villages, partly reflecting the disruptions of the ranking order brought about by the land reform, the importance attaching to notions of "the family's place in the village" has diminished with the years. Now, a generation after the disappearance of the landlord-tenant system, the status rankings which were sustained by that system are becoming a thing of the distant past. Even more is this the case in urban areas.

The decline in consciousness of family status is linked to the diminished authority of the househead, once the representative of the *ie* and leader of the family. Today, a third of a century after the term "househead" disappeared from the statutes, Japanese families have generally ceased to be authoritarian families. The change in terminology has reflected a crumbling of the preeminence of the patriarch, of the father, and of men in general. In the change from a male-dominated family based on the parent-child relationship to one based on the marital relationship and predicated on the principle of sexual equality, there has been a general rise in the position of women. The joke that two things have got tougher since the war, stockings and women, is not entirely mistaken. Sexual equality has certainly not been achieved in practice, but at least in the family women's position is far higher than it was in the prewar period.

Hence, too, marriage has also changed. Before the war, women married in the best interest of their *ie* and were described as *yome*—elder son's wife—and were indeed expected to be *yome* to their new family more than they were expected to be wives to their husbands. Now, far more importance is placed on understanding between the marital partners themselves, and this alone counts as a tremendous change. Even today, except in the large cities, more mar-

126

riages are made by arranged *miai* meetings than "for love," but it is now the usual practice for the *miai* to be followed by a period of dating after the engagement is made—an enormous difference from the days when it was not uncommon for husband and wife to speak to each other for the first time after the wedding ceremony. The honeymoon, which was once only for a limited social stratum, is now the general practice even in rural areas, something one could not have foreseen thirty years ago.

At the same time the number of girls in higher education steadily increases; the proportion going to high school is slightly higher than for boys, and at the university level the entrance ratios are getting close. Meanwhile, presumably as a result of increased employment, the age at first marriage, which was 23 for women some sixty years ago, has gone up to an average of 25.6. The age at first marriage for men has shown little change; at 28.3, the figure is not even a year more than what it was in the 1920s. This means the average age difference, which before the war was around four years, has decreased to 2.7 years, a change not unrelated to the changing character of the marital relationship.

It has also become the generally accepted view that in the towns it is better for a married couple to begin their life together living separately from their parents. Better-off families provide a separate house even if they do have the house room to accommodate an extra couple. It is also quite common to build a separate house in the garden adjoining the parents'. Lower down the income scale, where there is neither land nor money enough to provide the young couple with independent accommodation, it is common to rent rooms or an apartment apart from the parents. The trend toward the nuclear family is accelerated by these changes.

However, if one takes Japan as a whole, this new pattern

of establishing a new household with each marriage is not sufficiently widespread to be considered the dominant one. In rural areas it is still considered normal for an inheriting eldest son and his wife to live with the son's parents, and in the family enterprises in the cities, too, living together is usual, provided there is enough space in the parental home. But even in such cases the family life cycle differs from the prewar pattern (Morioka, 1973), and actual modes of living have changed. And although the postwar shortage of housing has passed, the still endemic conditions of cramped housing—the tiny "two rooms plus diner/kitchen" being still the norm—often impose space limits on the possibility of two married couples living together, and this, too—not just change in ideas—must be considered a factor promoting the nuclearization of the family in the cities.

In conjunction with these trends in marriage one needs to look at inheritance. The law has changed to a system of equal division among all children, but in fact property is not divided. Many parents still prefer the traditional pattern of passing on all their property to the eldest son, who in return accepts as a matter of course the obligation to care for them in their old age. This is especially clear in farm families, and is taken for granted in the older middle class of the towns, too—and is still accepted in the urban upper class. Even now a "successor" in that sense is still

Table 20 "Do You Revere Your Ancestors?" (percent)

	Yes	Not easy to say yes or no	Rather no than yes	Other; Don't know
1953	77	15	5	3
1973	67	21	10	2
1983	71	15	13	2

Source: The Institute of Statistical Mathematics, Kokuminsei Chōsa [Survey of the National Character].

considered necessary by over 60 percent of the population.

The percentage agreeing that "the idea that the eldest son should carry on the family and look after his parents is a good one" was around 40 percent both in a survey carried out by the Prime Minister's Office in 1955 and in an NHK survey twenty years later. A number of opinion surveys have found around 35 percent who think that the eldest son or "a succeeding son" should have a larger share of the inheritance (NHK, 1979a). Again, the Institute of Statistical Mathematics survey, summarized in Table 20, shows even now more than 70 percent who say that they revere their ancestors.

Thus, although one can certainly say that the prewar *ie* system has very largely disintegrated, the *ie* still nevertheless lives on in the idea that someone, even if it is not the *eldest* son, should carry on the *ie* inherited from the ancestors. One can reasonably say that the *ie* system still survives in this core idea.

However, even if the system does survive to some extent, the extended family ties which bound households in *dōzoku* groups have been notably weakened. Instead, the ties of personal blood relationships, which were formerly hidden under the relations of stem and branch families, have come to the surface. Personal ties between close and intimate relatives, meeting on a footing of equality and unconcerned about main or branch relationships or the nature of cousinships, have become the predominant form of kin ties, and as such they do not impose any of the constraints that the old extended family ties did before the war. This is particularly true of the families of wage or salary employees which have reinforced their independent character and become genuinely, as the Japanese phrase *maihōmu* suggests, refuges which individuals can think of as "my home."

CHAPTER 16

THE DISINTEGRATON OF LOCAL
COMMUNITIES

Rapid industrialization, accelerated change in agriculture, and the continuation of urbanization could not fail to bring great changes to the local communities of villages and urban wards—changes of such a magnitude as to make understandable that one should hear talk of neighborhood societies having "form but no content" or of "community disintegration" or "community dissolution."

Let us first consider the case of village society. We have already seen how farm families have differentiated into a small number of full-time farmers and a very large number of part-time farmers, with a concomitant increase in the number of non-farmers living in rural areas. Not a few former villages have become settlements of non-farmers in which a small number of farming families still survive—hence the common assertion that rural society has become a society of mixed settlement.

This is clearly shown in the survey of settlements conducted in parallel with the agricultural census which is summarized in Table 21. Between 1960 and 1980, the number of non-farmers grew from 25 out of an average settlement size of 64 households to 109 out of 141. These figures are slightly misleading since genuinely agricultural settlements, defined as those having more than 80 percent of their

Table 21   Occupational Composition of the Average Agricultural Settlement

	Full-time farmers	More than half income from agriculture	Up to half income from agriculture	Total agric. house-holds	Non-farming house-holds	Total house-holds
1960	13.4	13.0	12.5	39	25	64
1970	5.8	12.4	18.8	37	44	81
1980	4.4	7.1	21.5	33	109	141

Source: Calculated from the Nōgyō Shūraku Chōsa [Survey of Agricultural Settlements].

households engaged in agriculture, still made up more than half of the total number of settlements in 1970 and 35 percent in 1980: the averages in Table 21 are much influenced by the fact that there has been a vast inflow of non-agricultural commuters into former village settlements in the suburbs of the cities. However, this does not alter the fact that there has been a great increase in non-farming families so that now as many as 30 percent of settlements have only a minority of farmers. Add to this the fact that something approaching 70 percent of the so-called farming families derive more than half their income from outside agriculture and are approaching non-farmer status, and one gets a very clear picture of the rapidly growing heterogeneity of village society, a heterogeneity with clear implications for its social character.

To begin with, as a result of these structural changes, village society has lost the community-like character of a closed local society that it once had. Prewar villages were, to be sure, stratified into landlords and tenants and divided between those with and those without non-agricultural sources of income; they were not entirely homogeneous. Nevertheless, they were held together, under the leadership of the upper stratum of landlords or wealthier farmers, and

132

functioned as, in some degree, unitary organizations for the purposes of production and of daily social life. But today, long after the collapse of the landlord system, the differentiation between a small group of full-time farmers, keen to develop profitable production for the market, and a larger group of farmers who derive most of their income from outside farming and concentrate on self-sufficient production of their own rice, largely with an eye to security in their old age when they have retired from their non-agricultural jobs, makes it difficult for village communities to develop a sense of common purpose. There is also the question of leadership. Even after the land reform, up to the period of rapid growth, the farmers with large holdings had the income resources to give a lead to the village. Subsequently, as the proportion of part-time farmers has increased, the so-called one-acre farmers—a word which once described the poorest stratum of practically destitute villagers—have acquired, if not more wealth, at least more income than the farmers with big holdings, and the latter have lost their automatic preeminence. In addition, the increase in the number of non-farmers who commute from the villages because they cannot afford houses in the towns has made it even more difficult to contain the life of the residents in anything like the confines of the village, or to retain the semblance of a solidary community.

Secondly, in addition to this internal differentiation, the villages' links with outside society have been strengthened externally, too, compared with before the war, and the average villager's lifesphere has been vastly widened. The switch from the bicycle to the automobile widens it even further; the development of production for the market and the rise in the standard of living widen and deepen ties with the town, while everyday contacts are further multiplied through the commuting of the part-time farmers and the non-agricultural households. The local administration

133

reforms of 1953 rearranged and amalgamated the local government units which had existed since 1889, creating new units several times larger than the old ones and absorbing many rural settlements as suburbs within a local government area dominated by a central town and sharing the same administrative structure with urban areas. This has further strengthened contact between town and countryside and made the villages, no longer purely agricultural settlements, impossible to understand in isolation from the urban areas.

Further, as excessive concentration of industry begins to bring the disadvantages of over-density rather than the economies of concentration, factories begin to move out of the traditional industrial areas and seek to create new ones. So-called regional development of this kind decisively alters the structure of the villages in the regions affected, diluting if not destroying their character as agricultural settlements. Even apart from these planned regional developments, the prospects of cheap wage-labor and low land prices bring small individual factories into rural areas throughout the country, with similar results. Much the same consequences follow from urban housing sprawl, as high land prices force those who cannot afford houses in the city centers into new housing developments in suburban areas.

These structural changes in village society vary, of course, from region to region, but nowhere can one find any longer the village communities of former times. As communities, the villages are in the process of dissolution, and the traditional groupings within them no longer hold the same constraining force as they once had. The small neighborhood group—the *kumi*—which once had important functions in every sphere of life are being reduced to mere end-of-the-line units of the local administration; the funeral *kumi* no longer function as widely in providing mutual help in dealing with bereavement; religious belief and activity have declined, and with the opportunities for recreation becoming now a daily matter, the religious *kō* and the communal eating and drinking which accompanied their activities are now but shadowy relics of what they once were. Among the organizations which were created by the administration after the nineteenth-century local government system was established, two in particular, the youth group and the women's group, now have much reduced functions, and the youth groups, in fact, often find it difficult even barely to survive as organizations. The youth sections and women's sections of agricultural cooperatives which tended to replace the older organizations after the war also find it hard to remain active, and the local hamlet subdivisions of the cooperative become much restricted in their effectiveness with the increasing heterogeneity of farming units. Specialist cooperatives, within the general agricultural cooperatives, which arrange for communal marketing of fruit, of dairy products, or of poultry or silk cocoons, are generally organized among the specializing farmers of an area wider than a single village and hence are no longer organizations *of* the village. The days when all the farmers in a village, irrespective of whether they were full-time or part-time, acted together over a whole range of cooperative activities, which closely constrained the independence of all who live in the village, have long since passed.

The weakening of the constraints of the local community is not just a village phenomenon. In town neighborhoods, where those constraints had in any case been weaker, their loosening has gone further. To start with, urban growth has meant the development of a large number of new town neighborhoods which never had any community tradition in the first place.

Rapid economic growth and urbanization have also changed the structure of cities. Family commercial enterprises have come to be overwhelmed by the growth in

135

numbers of the new middle class and workers. The number of small family factory enterprises scattered among the residential areas has also diminished, and those which remain are full of anxieties about their future. Consequently, the owners of these family enterprises, in commerce or manufacturing, have far less ability to lead and control the affairs of their neighborhood than they had before the war. Even in the oldest *shitamachi* part of Tokyo, the urban neighborhoods retain very little of their former neighborhood community character, and in any case such neighborhoods, once considered typical of the pattern of Japanese urban life, are so no longer.

The new town dwellers who have been called into existence by rapid economic growth, the workers and the new middle class, have sought their housing either in the small private apartment blocks which have sprung up indiscriminately both in the older town areas and in the suburbs, or in the new housing estates either of individual houses or of massive apartment blocks. In neither case are they subject of the control of the older middle class. People paying relatively high rents to live in a wood-frame apartment block have no interest whatever in their local neighborhood and are concerned only to escape from it as soon as possible. The dwellers on the new estates are quite beyond the reach of the "men of influence" of the local community that might have been there before the estate. In the apartment block estates in particular the new residents often form Estate Self-Governing Associations rather different from the old neighborhood associations, and although they will express their relatively strong sense of citizens' rights when acting collectively to demand various environmental improvements from the local authority, when it comes to matters of daily life, freedom and individualistic diversity prevail. There is little question of constraining bonds of a community character.

So, in both city and countryside, it is far harder to get local neighborhoods to pull together than it was before the war. But the disappearance of these communitarian pressures and the undemocratic constraints they implied has meant at the same time that residents become more egoistic in their behavior and less willing to join together in cooperative activity. That is why for the last fifteen years one has heard people talking of the need to create not *kyōdōtai*—the Japanese word that we have translated here as "community"—but *komyuniti*. The word "community" first became a technical term and a subject for scholarly analysis with Robert MacIver's *Community: A Sociological Study*, published in 1917. There is nothing in that concept as developed since MacIver which requires neighborhood communities to be democratic. In modern Japan, however, after the weakening of the solidary bonds of the old *un*democratic community, the feeling that it is necessary to find new ways of organizing urban residents democratically, new ways of evoking a sense of citizen solidarity and cooperation, is expressed by using the borrowed foreign word. The demand for a new *komyuniti* shows just how far the decline of community has gone in Japan's towns and villages.

PART III

CONTEMPORARY JAPANESE SOCIETY

CHAPTER 17

THE STRUCTURE OF CONSCIOUSNESS

Already a third of a century has passed since the defeat, the second "opening of the country." Those thirty years have brought the great changes which I described in Part II. They were changes of a kind which, as they contemplated their devastated country immediately after the war, no Japanese ever anticipated. They were changes, therefore, which could not fail to bring about great changes in outlook.

We must remember, however, that in general, changes in material culture, guided only by criteria of efficiency, occur far more rapidly than changes in institutional culture or intellectual culture which are not transformed overnight. People's ideas and attitudes and character are affected by changes in their social environment, but the basic structure of consciousness is slow to change.

As a consequence, when violent social change occurs, quite big differences can appear between the generation which was already mature and subsequent generations which grew up in the changed environment. Those born in the early years of the century who were already adult at the time of the war, those who were still children when the war ended, and those who have been born and brought up since the war have therefore been differently affected by the postwar changes; they are in some senses different kinds of Japanese. Already, however, 80 percent of the population was born since 1925 and about a half since the end of the war. Consequently, even if the basic social character of the nation remains the same, the passage of generations should have wrought discernible alterations. It is common to speak of the prewar, the wartime, and the postwar generations, and, as we shall see, fairly clear differences can be discerned between those who were young children at the end of the war, those who were born in the 1930s, and those older generations who were born before that. In this sense, one can say that contemporary Japanese exhibit a complex transitional social character, differently affected by postwar social change while still retaining some traditional characteristics.

Here, rather than attempting a detailed analysis of the various generations, I shall give an overall picture of contemporary attitudes and values and subsequently amend this with a few remarks about outstanding differences between the generations.

We have already seen that the *ie*, the village, and the urban neighborhood structures which formerly molded and constrained the development of individual characters have been shaken loose, weakened, and partly broken down. The status order has crumbled. And this has affected character. Whereas formerly children grew up concerned with appearances and *giri* obligations, developing their moral ideas under the constant admonition: "Don't do that or people will laugh at you, you will lose face," nowadays, even if they still unconsciously react in a similar way when bringing up their own children, at least at the level of consciousness people have come to reject such principles. So, for instance, in the surveys of national character conducted by the Institute of Statistical Mathematics, when people were asked to agree or disagree with the statement "It is important to teach one's children not to be too concerned about matters of 'face' and prestige," the 40 percent who agreed in 1953 had grown to 70 percent twenty years later (NHK, 1979a).

Nevertheless one must set against this the answers to questions about *giri* obligations and *ninjō* personal relations—the words used to describe those interpersonal ties seen by Japanese intellectuals as the emotional basis for a peculiarly Japanese form of particularism. The number of people who will agree in such surveys that "nowadays far too many people take *giri* and *ninjō* much too lightly" usually runs at about 40 percent, and there has even been a decrease in the number of people who consider it superstitious to continue some of the traditional practices associated with the old lunar calendar like not holding funerals on *tomobiki* (friend-inviting) days or not holding weddings on *butsumetsu* (Buddha's passing) days. Most people are of the opinion that these are social customs that one cannot do much about. Another pertinent piece of evidence is provided by the question which has been asked on every occasion in the Institute of Statistical Mathematics surveys: "If you think what you want to do is right, do you think you should just go ahead and do it even if it offends against social custom, or do you think it's safer to follow custom?" As Table 22 shows, something like a third of the respondents had thought it safer to follow custom from the very first survey onward, but in the seventh survey in 1983 that figure rose almost 40 percent, and the number who think one should press for one's own ideas fell from 40 to 30 percent. The "superior force of custom" has not diminished. To put the matter in terms popularized by David Riesman (1950), Japanese, even in the modern period, were tradition-oriented types, and now in the postwar period, instead of maturing into inner-directed types they have changed to other-direction.

Table 22   "Should One Follow Custom?" (percent)

	Do what you think right	Follow custom	Depends on circum-stances	Other; Don't know
1953	41	35	19	5
1958	41	35	19	5
1963	40	32	25	3
1968	42	34	20	4
1973	36	32	29	4
1978	30	42	24	4
1983	29	39	29	3

Source: The Institute of Statistical Mathematics, Kokuminsei Chōsa [Survey of the National Character].

As far as family life is concerned, while preserving a certain attachment to the idea of the *ie* in spite of the dissolution of the *ie* system, most people are primarily concerned about the family in the sense of their individual household. They look forward simply to enjoying peaceful and affectionate relationships in *maihōmu*. Table 23 summarizes another of the results of the national character surveys. When offered a number of alternative answers to a question about the guiding principles of life, the number choosing "to live according to one's own taste, not being too much concerned about money or fame" or "to live cheerfully from day to day" was 32 percent in 1953 but had increased to 61 percent thirty years later, while the number who chose "to live a pure and just life, cutting one's way through all the wrongs and injustices of society" fell from 29 percent to 11 percent. (I have included in Table 23 some data from prewar surveys of young adults. They need to be discounted, especially the 1940 one, for the fact that people gave answers that were expected of them—a *tatemae* Sunday-best opinion rather than a *honne* cry from the heart—but even so the differences are unmistakable). The NHK attitude surveys have produced somewhat similar findings when,

Table 23 Guiding Principles of Life (percent)

	Becoming rich	Making one's name	Suiting one's own taste	Living cheerfully	Pure and just life	Serving society	Others; Don't know
1931	14	9	12	4	32	24	–
1940	9	5	5	1	41	30	–
1953	15	6	21	11	29	10	8
1958	17	3	27	18	23	6	6
1963	17	4	30	19	18	6	6
1968	17	3	32	20	17	6	5
1973	14	3	39	23	11	5	5
1978	14	2	39	22	11	7	5
1983	18	2	38	23	9	5	6

Sources: For 1953–78, the Institute of Statistical Mathematics, Kokuminsei Chōsa [Survey of the National Character]. For 1931, Sōtei Shisō Chōsa [Conscription Medical Examinations: Beliefs]; for 1940, Sōtei Kyōiku Chōsa Tokubetsu Chōsa [Conscription Medical Examination: Education, Special Survey].

in the analysis, respondents are divided into the "socially oriented" who are concerned about society and the "private-life oriented" who are more concerned about their personal affairs, the former number no more than 10 percent. The latter are further divided into the *maihōmu* type who place great value on the family doing things together rather than each individually doing his own thing, and the individualistic type who think it important that the family should not always be together but that each individual should have some time to himself. The former account for 50 and the latter for 28 percent (NHK, 1985).

The majority of Japanese, therefore, are *maihōmu* types who give priority to private life, but in a society in which employees predominate as much as in the present one, *maihōmu* is supported by work in the workplace. And while the workplace is no longer characterized by familistic groupism to the same degree as before the war, neverthe-

145

less a great deal of that spirit is alive and well. In the immediate postwar period, Japanese enterprise familism was generally thought, under the influence of American management theory, to be premodern and in need of amendment. All kinds of new forms of enterprise training and personnel management were imported with weird Japan-English labels, but the basic character of the system survived. It served, moreover, to promote the expansion of enterprises and the rapid growth of the economy. And that in turn has meant that the familistic groupism which was once exposed to modernistic criticism has once again found spokesmen who confidently praise its virtues.

The NHK Broadcast Culture Research Institute surveyed The attitudes and values of the Japanese four times between 1973 and 1988. One of the techniques employed was to ask people to divide their relationships in their residential neighborhood and in their workplace into the following three categories: formal (exchanging greetings or interacting only in matters where work is directly involved); partial (being able to chat in a fairly relaxed manner, talking or eating

Table 24   Desirable Patterns of Relations (percent)

	Formal		Partial		Total	
	1973	1978	1973	1978	1973	1978
Neighbor relations	15	15	50	53	35	32
Workplace relations	11	10	26	31	59	55
	Formal		Partial		Total	
	1983	1988	1983	1988	1983	1988
Neighbor relations	20	19	48	53	32	27
Workplace relations	14	15	32	38	52	45

Source: NHK Public Opinion Research Institute, Nihonjin no Ishiki Chōsa [Survey of Attitudes and Values of the Japanese].

and drinking together after work); and total (being able to discuss and help each other over anything and everything) (NHK, 1985). Table 24 shows what people say is their preferred pattern. Those who would like to have total relationships with their workmates are decreasing but still number close to one half; partial relationships are preferred with neighbors. These results reflect the dissolution of neighborhood communities and the growing relative importance of the workplace in the live of the Japanese people today. While attitudes toward work and neighborhood relations are changing, Japan can be called a workplace-centered society, and it is on success or failure in the workplace that the chance of *maihōmu* being a happy home depends.

And in the workplace, traditional familistic relationships are still very much alive. In the Institute of Statistical Mathematics survey, people were asked to choose whether they would prefer "a department chief who never expects you to work beyond what the regulations call for, but who never looks after you in matters not related to your work" or "a department chief who sometimes expects far more work than you are supposed to do but who cares about what happens to people and looks after them in matters that have nothing to do with work." In repeated surveys since 1953, an overwhelming 80 percent majority have consistently chosen the second, and in 1983 the figure reached 89 percent. A similar question in the NHK survey produced 70 percent who preferred to work with someone who was easy to get along with even if not of the highest ability, rather than someone who was of outstanding ability but hard to get along with, and the analysis suggested that the Japanese people were still more oriented to emotion-laden relationships than to ability and noted that Japanese enterprises were still very much concerned to evoke the spirit of harmony and general cooperativeness.

However, if these findings are considered in relation to

147

others of the questions asked, it appears that the numbers oriented to ability and those oriented to emotion-laden relations are fairly evenly balanced, and also that there is a difference between the generations. If one takes the question about the desirable pattern of relationships, the breakdowns suggest that it is the older generations who are the "wet" ones leaning toward total relationships, while the younger age groups are more "dry," tending to partial relations.

Again, in the familistic groupism of the workplace, it is true that the total-group principle still lives on in the labor movement, uniting both blue and white collar workers in a single enterprise union and providing, in the possibility of a noncontradictory double loyalty to both firm and union, one of the conditions for Japan's economic advance —one of the conditions promoting whole-hearted devotion to one's work. But one should not overlook the fact that in recent years people have been less inclined to live like bees, devoting their whole lives to work. A Prime Minister's Office survey showed that in 1955 50 percent of respondents said that they hoped to work harder than other people (rather more than said they thought it enough to work as hard as other people), some twenty years later, in 1977, the proportion giving the second reply had increased to 75 percent. NHK surveys show that there were 40 percent who were oriented to giving work priority, over 25 percent who were in favor of giving equal weight to work and leisure, and 30 percent who would give priority to leisure (NHK, 1979a, 1985). In another NHK survey on work attitudes, which asked whether people thought they were serving their company or organization even to the extent of sacrificing their personal lives, 69 percent altogether said "yes"—25 percent "definitely yes," and 44 percent "well, I suppose you could say so." But when the question was: "Do you find the things most worth living for in your work or outside your work?" the 54 percent majority who said "work"

148

Table 25   Feelings toward the Emperor (percent)

	Rever-ence	Good will	Indiffer-ence	Resent-ment	Other; Don't know
1973	33.3	20.3	42.7	2.2	1.4
1978	30.2	21.9	44.1	2.4	1.5
1983	29.3	20.9	46.4	2.2	1.3
1988	27.5	22.1	46.5	2.1	1.9

Source: NHK Broadcast Culture Research Institute, Nihonjin no Ishiki Chō-sa [Survey of Attitudes and Values of the Japanese].

in 1967 had shrunk to 46 percent in 1974 and 37 percent in 1978 (NHK, 1979b).

However, it is safe to say, at any rate, that contemporary Japanese in general live for their family and their work and are not very concerned about outside society. With the dissolution of the familistic state the sense of loyalty to the state has also been weakened. Those who thought that "for the country to prosper, it can't be helped if individual freedom has sometimes to be sacrificed" still numbered more than 50 percent in 1956, but less than 30 percent in 1975. And the Emperor whom, before the war, more than 80 percent of the people thought of as a god or at least as a being beyond the sphere of ordinary humans, has become, as Table 25 shows, someone who evokes no feelings at all in nearly half the population—even if 28 percent still say they revere him and another 22 percent bear him good will. The older generation are overwhelmingly of the opinion that an emperor as a symbol of the nation is a very good thing to have, whereas in the younger age strata, around 30 percent say either that it makes no difference whether there is an emperor or not or else that a republic would be better. A composite analysis of a number of surveys suggests that 1933 is the transitional birth date. Among those born before that date, a majority express reverence for the Emperor; among those born later, the indifferent predominate. This suggests that as time goes on the indifferent group will gain overall dominance—a vast change when one recalls the prewar period when the existence of the Emperor was an unquestioned absolute.

CHAPTER 18

THE STRATIFICATION SYSTEM OF CONTEMPORARY JAPAN

One element of the Japanese class structure was removed after the war—the landlord class. Landlords had gradually lost their importance with the development of a capitalist economy, and by the 1930s they could no longer be spoken of as part of a ruling class, but nevertheless the disappearance of the landlords was a significant event; postwar Japan could never be the same as prewar Japan.

However, the class structure immediately after the defeat was still not very different from what it had been: family enterprises, the so-called old middle class, made up nearly 60 percent of the working population. Table 26 summarizes the census results to show changes in the class structure. In 1950, production workers accounted for only 20 percent and salaried workers only a little more than 10 percent. But, as we have already seen, subsequent changes and especially the annual decrease in agricultural workers has reduced family enterprises to 23 percent and expanded the working class to 70 percent, thus reversing the proportions between employees and family workers. Salaried workers doubled their proportion from one-tenth to one-quarter, and production workers increased from 20 to almost 30 percent. Non-production workers in commerce and services tripled their share of the total.

Table 26   The Japanese Class Structure (percent)

	1950	1955	1965	1975	1985
Capitalist class	1.9	2.0	3.6	5.9	5.8
Family enterprisers	58.9	53.2	38.3	29.4	23.3
Farming, forestry, and fishing workers	44.6	37.7	23.0	12.7	8.3
Sales and service	7.1	8.5	7.8	7.8	6.7
Professional, and technical workers	1.0	0.9	1.2	2.1	2.7
Working class	38.2	43.6	56.9	63.3	69.5
Salaried employees	11.9	12.5	17.0	21.3	24.5
Production workers	20.0	22.4	29.2	28.2	28.5
Non-production workers	4.3	6.8	9.3	11.5	13.0

Source: For 1950–65, Ohashi, 1971; for 1975 and 1985, calculated from National Census.

So we get the following picture of the class structure of contemporary Japan: at the peak a handful of members of the capitalist class, then the old middle class stratum of family enterprises made up of under 10 percent of farmers and somewhat less in the commercial and service trades, the new middle class of the approximately 25 percent salaried workers and a small number of professional and technical workers, and finally the 40 percent who are workers.

However, these figures are arrived at simply by mechanically adding the categories of the census, and they do not necessarily tell us a great deal about reality. For example, the group included in the capitalist class increased from 2 to 6 percent, but this category includes a number of people who have become company directors simply because the family enterprise has been turned into a public company for tax advantage purposes. The family enterprisers category is also very diverse, and some within this category have incomes well below those of salaried employees. Again, when one speaks of the capitalist class, one has to remember that the majority of modern enterprises are run by professional managers. The dissolution of the prewar *zaibatsu* after the war greatly reduced the importance of real capitalists, even though the companies involved have regrouped again. According to a study of the Japanese business elite (Mannari, 1965), the number of professional bureaucratic managers, which had been about 20 percent of the total before 1910 and over 40 percent in the 1920s, had reached more than 70 percent by 1960, far exceeding in number the 10 percent of original founders of their firms and the nearly 20 percent who had inherited a family firm. In the working class, too, in spite of the convergence of income between salaried and production workers to the point that people speak of a "grey collar" class, there is still a division between the two. The broad division into three classes, then, conceals a large number of complexities.

Consequently, here, too, as when treating the prewar period, I shall treat this class structure as a basis but look in more detail at the stratification system.

To begin with the elite who control Japan, they can be seen as made up of the small handful of managers who run not the small and medium enterprises but the large monopoly firms. Private firms with paid-up capital of over a billion yen number 2,350, or less than 0.2 percent of the total number of enterprises. But they have 65 percent of the total paid-up capital. It is the men who run these mammoth firms who control Japan, and together with the conservative politicians and senior bureaucrats they make up contemporary Japan's ruling stratum.

The middle stratum, by contrast, consists of the owners of small and medium businesses, the supervisory and managerial workers at the top of the white collar hierarchy, and the new type of family enterprisers, namely professional and technical workers. This new middle stratum has lost much of the subordinate local leadership role once played by the older middle strata, and it has been reduced in size with the disappearance of the landlords. Nevertheless, the owners of small and medium businesses do play a mediating role, representing the interest of their localities vis-à-vis those with political power. And the upper white collar workers often play a brokering role linking the large enterprises with the small ones that subcontract for them. In those senses one can see some continuity with the prewar period.

But in spite of these structural features, in general, the intermediate stratum has declined in importance, and its grip on the lower subordinate strata has been weakened. To that extent the ruling stratum has to operate more direct control over the subordinate masses, but they too have not only grown in number but become more complex in structure.

Farmers, for instance, as already described, are differentiated into the less than 10 percent of *jiritsu nōka*—those getting an acceptable minimum income from full-time farming; those with some other stable employment—landowning workers with a relatively affluent living standard; and a much less fortunate third group who fall into neither category. One can hardly talk about farmers as a homogeneous stratum. The family enterprisers in the towns are equally heterogeneous. Even if one leaves out of account, as being properly in the middle stratum, those who are capable of dominating their locality, the others can be divided into a group who have a relatively stable income and a floating group who barely manage to survive in a situation of great insecurity with frequent bankruptcies and fresh starts. Among the new majority of wage workers, although the wage differential between the workers in the large firms and those in the medium and tiny enterprises has narrowed since the prewar period, the differences are still too great to consider them a single stratum. Again, the recent tendency is for the increase in production workers to fall off, or even to begin to reverse itself, the increase being now seen in the non-production workers in sales and services. The latter make up a growing proportion of the working class, and they, too, are differentiated into many types and cannot simply be lumped together with blue collar workers. Even if the non-manual workers, including government workers, are not so far removed from blue collar workers in terms of their objective economic position, nevertheless they have a white collar consciousness and that makes a difference.

In spite of this diversity of the lower subordinate strata, one thing they have in common is that their living standards have risen considerably since before the war, and although in social structural terms the intermediate strata have diminished and the subordinate strata have increased, in terms of consciousness and subjective perceptions, a large proportion of those in the subordinate classes, reflecting this new prosperity, see themselves as belonging to a "middle class," even though they are a long way from being a middle class in any strict sense. A number of postwar surveys have asked people to assign "your family's level of living" to one of the categories shown in Table 27. The Prime Minister's Office's Survey of the People's Livelihood has been conducted every year since 1958 with the exception of 1962–63, and as the table shows, the proportion who put themselves in the middle middle category started off as less than 40 percent but gradually increased until in 1979 it had reached over 60 percent. The year 1980, and the fall in real wages in that year, caused a certain erosion from middle-class to lower-middle class consciousness, but still the middle middles were in a majority. If one adds the upper and lower middles, ever since about 1970, the apogee of the rapid growth period, with certain fluctuations, the vast

Table 27 Subjective Perceptions of Social Stratal Membership (percent)

	Upper	Upper middle	Middle middle	Lower middle	Lower
1958	11	3	37	32	17
1965	5	7	50	30	8
1975	5	7	59	23	5
1985	0.2	6	52	29	9

Source: Prime Minister's Office, Kokumin Seikatsu Chōsa [Survey of the People's Livelihood].

	Upper	Upper middle	Lower middle	Upper lower	Lower lower	Don't know; No answer
1955	0.2	7.1	34.8	37.7	18.6	1.6
1965	0.3	12.1	42.7	32.2	8.8	3.9
1975	1.2	22.9	52.7	17.3	4.1	1.8
1985	1.9	24.0	47.3	17.5	5.9	3.4

Source: National Committee for Research on Social Stratification and Mobility.

majority—about 90 percent—of Japanese have thought of themselves as belonging to the middle class.

In terms of subjective perceptions, there is no doubt that the intermediate strata have grown enormously. The same conclusion emerges from the studies of social stratification and mobility which have been conducted as a proj-

Table 28 Sense of Class Membership (percent)

	Capitalist class	Middle propertied class	Working class
1955	1.4	23.1	75.5
1960	3.4	31.4	65.2
1975	4.9	24.1	71.0
1985	4.7	28.5	66.8

Source: Tominaga, 1979. p. 385; for 1985, National Committee for Research on Social Stratification and Mobility.

ect of the Japanese Sociological Association since 1955 (Tominaga, 1979). But that survey also asked another question:"If you were to divide the nation into the working class, the *chūsan-kaikyū* (the middle property-owning class), and the capitalist class, which would you say you belonged to?" Then, as Table 28 shows, 70 percent put themselves in the working class. And, in spite of 80 percent of respondents counting themselves as in the middle (if one includes the lower middles and the upper middles), when the question is put in the stratal terms of the earlier question, only a quarter assign themselves to the middle property-owning class. There is a big gap in perceptions here which is one clue to the understanding of contemporary Japanese politics.

What I mean is this: the great majority of those who consider themselves as working class when asked about classes see themselves as the middle stratum when the question is posed in stratal terms. With their consumption levels continuing to rise, they close their eyes to the imbalances and insecurities of their lives and bask in the illusion of being middle class persons. The proportion who count themselves as belonging to the middle property-owning class is also rather larger than the facts of the situation support, if one counts as properly belonging to that class only those households with a sufficient basis of security to overcome unexpected misfortunes. (For example, the savings survey of the Management and Coordination Agency found that the average household even in the top 20 percent, with [in 1984] an annual income of 10.52 million yen, had savings of only 16.22 million and debts of 5.10 million.) But that aside, when those who hesitate to call themselves members of the middle property-owning class and count themselves as working class still perceive themselves as "middle class," it is likely that this will be reflected in support for conservative parties in elections.

We should not forget, however, that in spite of this growingly dominant middle-class consciousness, almost 10 percent of the population still consider themselves as belonging to the lower, or lower lower, class. These are the least fortunate citizens at the very bottom of Japanese society, the welfare recipients who make up 2.1 percent of households and 1.2 percent of the population, plus the border-line group who are in constant danger of falling into the welfare-recipient category. These are the people who have not only not benefited from the rapid growth of the Japanese economy, but have also suffered most directly from its side effects.

CHAPTER 19

THE CONSERVATIVE–RADICAL PARADOX

Japanese politics went through a turbulent period in the dramatic changes which followed immediately on the defeat. The prewar Seiyūkai and Minseitō were reconstituted under new names as conservative parties, but the new radical parties which had had little strength to speak of in the prewar period suddenly blossomed under the democratization policies of the Occupation army. If only for a brief space of time, there was even a coalition government uniting the Socialist Party with one of the conservative parties. However, as already mentioned, Occupation policy changed its basic thrust: the concern to conduct an "experiment in democracy" gave way to plans for turning Japan into an anti-communist bastion. So, after the failure of the coalition government and the overwhelming victory of the Liberal Party in the subsequent 1949 elections, political power in Japan was directed toward the restructuring of the democratic system created by the new constitution in such a way as to "adapt it to Japanese traditions and circumstances." This was the so-called reverse course period, with the conservative parties adopting the reactionary posture of "radical" transformation of the system, and as a consequence the radical parties seeking to "conserve" the system based on the new constitution.

This political situation was further consolidated when the rival radical and then the rival conservative parties amalgamated, and thus the basic fabric of postwar politics was created—what is sometimes called "the 1955 system," since that was the year in which the amalgamation occurred. When the wartime single party—the Imperial Rule Assistance Association—disintegrated with the defeat, there followed a decade of multiparty politics of great complexity. Both on the Right and on the Left there was continuous fission and fusion which was accelerated by the purging of wartime leaders from civic life and the subsequent revocation of those purge orders. That period came to an end in 1955. It was then that the divided Socialist Party once again reunited, and this was an additional factor precipitating the amalgamation of the conservative parties to form the Liberal Democratic Party. In the background to this unification of the conservative parties was pressure from big business, feeling its muscle after the "Special Procurement Boom" brought by American purchases during the Korean War, and now ready to play its part as leading

Table 29 Distribution of Seats in the Lower House of the Diet

Election year/month	Liberal Democratic	So- cialist	Demo- cratic Socialist	Clean Govt.	Com- munist	New Liberal Club
1958 May	287	166			1	
1960 Nov.	296	145	17		3	
1963 Nov.	283	144	23		5	
1967 Jan.	277	140	30	25	5	
1969 Dec.	288	90	31	47	14	
1972 Dec.	271	118	19	29	38	
1975 Nov.	249	123	29	55	17	17
1979 Oct.	253	107	36	58	41	4
1980 June	286	107	33	34	29	12
1983 Dec.	250	112	38	58	26	8
1986 July	300	85	26	56	26	6

Note: Non-party independents omitted.

actor in the economy's turn from reconstruction to growth. The year 1955 was also when the White Paper on the Economy declared that "the postwar period is over" and introduced the term "technological innovation" into the vocabulary of daily discourse as it spelled out its vision of the possibilities of future growth.

Thus Japanese politics, as the economy entered the period of rapid growth, took shape as a two-party system, with opposition between a conservative and a radical party. More accurately, it could be spoken of as a one-and-a-half party system in terms of the relative strength of the parties, both then and for many years after. The conservative party maintained overwhelming control, and under its dominance the radical party could do little more than retain the one-third share of seats necessary to prevent amendment of the constitution. And within this relatively unchanging balance of forces, it was not the majority ruling party but the minority opposition party which was subject to fission. Out of its declining strength the Clean Government Party was born, and the Communist Party grew to be a significant force, producing a multi-party Left, a situation which served only further to strengthen the power of the dominant conservative majority.

Japanese politics in this period of conservative dominance was basically revisionist—looking toward revision of the new constitution when opportunity should arise, while conserving the Japanese-American security system. This basic character was never more clearly revealed than in 1960 at the time of the renewal of the Security Treaty with the United States. But revisionist tendencies at least were held back by the mass outburst of popular feeling at that time in reaction against the attempt to force the treaty through the Diet by undemocratic means. Thereafter, the single-minded pursuit of economic growth through technological innovation—while lauding the effectiveness of the Security Treaty system—has been what conservative politics have been all about. These policies have seen the expansion of the national product steadily continue: national income has grown and living levels have risen. And the social structure has vastly changed as a result: industrialization has been "radically" promoted.

Against the background of these structural changes, the 1960s were, for Japanese politics, a period of peaceful calm. The mechanisms of conservative control over rural areas, one of their main bases of support, remained intact, and similar mechanisms prevailed in the older urban areas with heavy concentrations of family enterprises. By contrast, among the workers on whose support the radical parties depended, there was growing apathy and alienation from party politics. In the absence of any coming together of the labor union federations, there was no reason to expect any crumbling of the conservative structure of power.

The conservative party's stronghold, its private fief, was the countryside. After the land reform, the villages could never be the same as they had been before. No longer were the voters prepared automatically to vote for the candidates their landlord supported. That mechanism ceased to work. But still the great majority of farmers' votes were given to conservative candidates, and the villages remained a conservative stronghold. But it was a stronghold which required a great deal of money to keep in good repair. Whereas before the war one could keep a political base entirely secure simply by getting a hold over a small handful of landlords, after the war the stratum of "influential men" with whom it was necessary to maintain good contacts was immeasurably wider. Only if a whole host of opinion leaders of greater or lesser influence were prepared to say that your election was in the local interest—that you would get roads and bridges built or repaired, that you would secure grants and subsidies or authorizations for local government loans—only with such support could you hope to get elected. Members of the Diet organized these opinion leaders into their personal Support Societies and had to devote endless care to nursing their constituencies. It was necessary to build up a follower network among the members of the prefectural assemblies and through them with village councillors. This required vast funds, which were obtained partly by the party itself from the special fund-raising organizations set up by big business, and partly by funds which individual politicians or their faction leaders collected from private firms. As a consequence, the main directions of policy inevitably follow the interests of the large corporations, and although the rural voters know this, nevertheless they follow the suasions of their local opinion leaders because they see it as the best way of serving local interests. Those local leaders—the village and town mayors, and councillors—repay the politician they favor by making sure that he receives a large vote in their town or village—a vote which puts them in a strong position to expect him to act as broker and supporter when they demand something of central government. This whole process strengthens the leadership position of the local influentials and gives them a very positive incentive to play an eager part in operating the politician's vote-collecting machine.

In the older-settled districts of the cities, too, some of the same sort of mechanisms operate. Given the general underdevelopment of municipal environment facilities in Japanese cities, there has been plenty of opportunity for direct "drains and dustbins" activity, of immediate benefit to local neighborhoods, for the local city and borough councillors to perform. Most of them are family enterprisers who live and work in the neighborhood; they, too, have direct links with metropolitan or prefectural assemblymen and through them with national politicians, links which help to consolidate their own position in their neighborhoods

163

as well as giving them the sort of satisfaction and feeling of self-importance that comes from a sense of being political actors, involved at the grass roots in the politics of the nation. They have to earn that sense of satisfaction by campaigning fiercely for the election of the politician who is at the head of their network. Thus, the older areas of the cities are very like the villages in being strong bases of conservative support.

But, as already noted, the bigger the city the weaker this base of conservative support. As the older type of urban society disintegrated with the steady increase in the proportions of wage and salary employees, the vote-collecting power of conservative politicians diminished. Nevertheless, it has not entirely disappeared, particularly in the provincial cities, and the shift in voting strength in the large cities does not have as great an influence on the whole political picture as it might, since the electoral system itself operates to give a greater weight to rural than to urban votes. Most of the urban areas outside of the big cities are, like rural areas, dominated by the conservatives: in fact, the further you go from the big cities the stronger conservative dominance, and therein lies a source of the Liberal Democratic Party's national strength.

By contrast, the radical opposition which has absorbed the mission of "conserving" the new constitutional structure has been unable to make an effective response. Not only has it been unable to break the conservative pattern of local government politics which depends on connections with the party in power, it has even failed to take full advantage of the expansion in their potential source of support—the growing number of wage and salary workers. When the 1955 structure was established, there was a general expectation that the Socialist Party would make rapid advances, but as the Liberal Democratic Party pursued its "radical" line of rapid economic growth, this expectation was betrayed. The Socialist Party's defense of the constitution, once its most fundamental political principle, lost much of its meaning as the Liberal Democratic Party abandoned concrete plans for constitutional reform. At the same time the doctrinaire belief that the Socialist Revolution would be brought about by increasing poverty was destroyed by the technological revolution and the high rate of growth. The Socialist Party was unable to devise a political program which responded to the social-structural changes which the accelerated pace of industrialization had brought, and it did not make adequate efforts to expand the basis of its support.

Immediately after the war, the majority of Diet members in the radical parties were members of the prewar socialist movement, but as time passed the majority came to be composed of former trade unionists who had moved late into politics. The trade unions had from the very beginning been the central base of support, but as the number of union politicians within the party increased, it gradually consolidated its character as a union party. But the unions were divided. Whereas the various bodies which provided money for conservative politicians, the Federation of Economic Organizations (Keidanren), the Japan Federation of Employers' Associations (Nikkeiren), the Japan Chamber of Commerce and Industry (Nisshō), and the Committee for Economic Development (Keizai Dōyūkai) all held identical views about politics and acted unitedly in concert, the various trade union federations—Sōhyō, Dōmei, and neutral Chūritsu Rōren, and Shinsanbetsu—were ideologically divided, and out of one of these divisions the Democratic Socialist Party separated from the Socialist Party. It is not surprising that with such a divided labor movement the radical parties found it difficult to counter a conservative party backed by a united business world.

Moreover, as economic growth proceeded, the workers

became more and more apathetic toward radical politics, more apathetic toward political parties in general. We have already seen that workers organized into enterprise unions were fundamentally oriented to their own enterprise, their own workshop, finding no contradiction in a dual loyalty to both enterprise and union. Such an orientation hardly leads to their giving united support to radical parties in their capacity as organized workers. Add to this that the unionization ratio has been falling and that 70 percent of workers are outside of the unions. There have been no signs of any strong impulse on the part of organized workers to join together with the unorganized in an attempt to take the mechanisms of conservative dominance apart. In fact, on the contrary, the gap between the labor movement, dominated by the government employees' unions, and the rest of the work force has been growing.

As a consequence, support for the Socialist Party has been at first stagnating and subsequently declining rather than increasing. The Socialist Party not only has been unable to extend its support among the workers, it has also failed to gain any support in rural areas in spite of the growingly divisive heterogeneity of the village population as economic growth proceeds: beyond vociferously demanding an increase in the price of rice in exactly the same way as the conservative politicians, it has had little to offer. As a union party, the Socialist Party was not ready in its policies or campaigns to sound warning bells about the way in which the socioeconomic structure was developing, and a party which was dominated by members of the Diet—a reverse-pyramid party with a narrow popular base—was not one which could change its doctrinaire party platform. This conservatism of the radical party was no match for the radicalism of the conservatives.

Thus the base of support for the Socialist Party which should have been the core of the radical opposition was not only narrowed by the defection of the Democratic Socialists but also threatened by the Communist Party, which recovered from the long period of stagnation brought on by its earlier extremist tactics and set about expanding its party organization. The urban stratum of old middle class voters, where it should also have been able to develop support, was captured by the Clean Government Party. In this way, instead of encroaching on the bases of the conservative party's power, the support for the radical parties became fractionated and eroded; a multiparty opposition was created.

CHAPTER 20

THE BASIS OF CONSERVATIVE POLITICS

The brief coalition mentioned in the previous chapter, uniting radical and conservative parties for seven months in 1948, represents the only break in a continuous postwar history of conservative governments. Already the Liberal Democratic Party has held power for a quarter of a century.

Support for conservative government has come from big business, which has contributed large sums in political donations and received in return large sums of government investment and a taxation system favoring business corporations. It has come also from the inhabitants of villages and the older urban wards—more especially the owners of small businesses and their families—who, in spite of the postwar erosion of local community sentiment, have nevertheless been induced by the mechanisms already described to vote for the conservative party as the party in power and the source of benefits. Another powerful factor in maintaining the status quo has been the electoral system itself: the boundaries, and the number of members (between three and five) elected from each constituency, have indeed been modified to take account of the massive flow of population into the large cities, but only to a minor degree, which has still left the rural areas considerably over-represented.

At the same time, it must not be forgotten that the reduction in the number of owners of family enterprises and the increase in wage employees—the near reversal of their proportions in the postwar years—does not necessarily mean an increase in support for the radical parties. We should not forget that while there are 70 percent of the population who are prepared to count themselves as members of the working class, the proportion who, in social stratum terms, would put themselves in the "middle middle" had reached 60 percent by the late 1970s—a steady increase from the 40 percent twenty years earlier. Add to these the nearly 10 percent who count themselves as upper middle and the more than 20 percent of lower middles, and the total is 90 percent. With such a change in self-perceptions going on, a radical party would have had to work very hard indeed to increase its support.

What is responsible for this steady growth of middle class consciousness? Undoubtedly, it is a consequence of rapid economic growth, of the fact that conservative governments' single-minded pursuit of national prosperity has, whatever one may think of its side effects, expanded the national income and raised levels of living.

Table 30   Consumption Levels (1980 = 100)

	Whole country	Non-farm families	Farm families
1965	59.0	61.9	46.4
1970	78.2	80.5	68.2
1975	92.9	90.6	90.0
1980	100.0	100.0	100.0
1985	105.4	104.9	107.4

Source: Management and Coordination Agency, Statistics Bureau, Annual, Report on Household Budgets.

The rapid growth of the Japanese economy has brought great changes to the traditional consumption patterns of the Japanese people. Once, in the prewar period, consumption was seen as something nnworthy, if not actually a vice. Today, if not exactly a virtue, and in spite of recent calls for the nation to conserve resources and energy, it is far from being seen as a sin. Thriftiness and the propensity to save remain strong, partly because social security levels are still low, but marketing techniques using the mass media have absorbed rising incomes, and as Table 30 shows, the standard of living has generally risen both in the cities and in the countryside. The change in rural areas is particularly striking: the tide of mass consumption has washed into the villages, too, as it has swept across the whole country.

After the defeat the standard of living fell far below pre-war levels. For a period it was close to half of what it had been in the late 1920s. In that period of food shortage—the bamboo-shoot period as it was called—it was all people could do, especially those in the towns, to find enough food to survive. Within ten years, however, living standards were back to prewar levels and thereafter rose rapidly. The Engel coefficient for the proportion of incomes spent on food, which had stood at 50 percent for farm families and 36 percent for urban worker families in 1935, had reached about 40 percent for both town and country in 1960; today it is 26 percent in worker families and 21 percent in farm families.

With this decline in the proportion of income spent on food, the structure of consumption began gradually to improve from about 1955. The marked spurt in economic activity which began in 1956, following on the postwar recovery, became known as the Jimmu boom—the greatest boom since the legendary Emperor Jimmu descended from heaven. What became known, extending the metaphor, as the Three Sacred Treasures—the television, the washing machine, and the refrigerator—soon became possessions to be taken for granted in ordinary households throughout the country. Styles of living were westernized, affecting

171

food, furniture, and clothing. By the 1970s the Three Sacred Treasures had given way to the Three Cs—car, color television, and cooler (air conditioner)—and automobile ownership spread rapidly. Even after the period of rapid growth was under way, few ever imagined that the proportion of car-owning families would reach the 67 percent that it stands at today. That is a measure of the speed with which the ownership of consumer durables has been diffused within a short space of time. Consumption reaches increasingly high levels and is increasingly diversified.

One of the standard categories used in family-budget analysis which has notably expanded according to government surveys, particularly in rural areas, is "miscellaneous expenditure." With the proportion of each age group going on from compuslory education to high school now reaching 95 percent, and university attendance approaching 40 percent of the age group, and with the increase in recreational expenditure, this increase is not surprising. Even if educational expenditures remain a considerable burden, nevertheless it has become commonplace to hope to send one's children to the university. Most people may still spend their days off for the most part resting at home or watching television, but there is a much greater tendency in recent years to seek more positive use of leisure. Although there has been some tendency for expenditure on tourism and recreation to decline since the oil crisis, recreational journeys involving at least one night away from home have now reached 1.4 per capita; over a third of the population take trips every year lasting more than four nights, and travel *en famille* is becoming increasingly common. The Surveys of the Peoples' Livelihood conducted by the Prime Minister's Office show the results of these changes. Although, since 1974, the numbers who think themselves worse off than the previous year have exceeded the number who think themselves better off, two-thirds reported no particular change, and the percentage who say that they are "satisfied with their present life" in 1985 was close to 70 percent. All this helps to explain why middle-class consciousness has grown in recent years and provided such infertile breeding soil for the desire to change the structure of conservative power established over so many years.

Thus, one-party rule by the Liberal Democratic Party has continued to the present day. It has been sustained by high levels of economic growth. However, even growth at such abnormal rates, whatever its effect in raising consumption levels, could not do much to raise the overall quality of life, affected as that was by the poverty of the nation's capital stock. This imbalance gave rise to what one might, with a certain amount of exaggeration, call a new sense of poverty. The man who owns a motor car which he uses only for Sunday drives might, for instance, live in a Housing Corporation apartment with two rooms and a diner/kitchen. Or someone living in a six-mat (12 square-meter), one-room private apartment might have such an array of consumer durables that he or she has hardly enough space to sleep. It was such imbalances that growth failed rapidly to cure. Although Japan reached the level of the other advanced countries in the diffusion of consumer durables, the poor quality of capital stock continued to reflect past poverty. Japan's housing capital has been estimated to be only one-tenth of America's and one-third that of West Germany. As a consequence, dissatisfaction with housing is strong and combines with the underdevelopment of environmental facilities, which we shall consider later, to breed a certain antipathy toward the government—not yet a desire to overturn the whole structure of conservative rule, but at least a sense of alienation. When one says that a widespread middle-class consciousness sustains conservative politics, one is talking only of passive support—of the absence of any positive impulse to resist the local conservative establishment in the villages and small towns and urban neighborhoods which, made up predominantly of the owners of family enterprises, provides the solid core of support for the government party. Moreover, since the ending of the high-growth period and the entry into a phase of lower growth rates, support for the conservative party has declined.

The votes received by the Liberal Democratic Party in elections for the House of Representatives fell below 50 percent in 1967, having been above 55 percent before that. Thereafter they have remained in the 40 percent range. It is particularly in the large cities that the Liberal Democrats' support has fallen. As a rough generalization, the larger the city the higher the proportion of wage and salary employees, and the less the ability of local politicians to collect votes even from the family proprietors as the smaller businessmen among them have broken away and been absorbed into the organizations of the Clean Government Party or the Communist Party. And so the Liberal Democrats' share of the votes started to decline from the end of the 1960s, and the decline became even more marked in the 1970s. To summarize the results of a variety of public opinion polls, one can say that the number of firm supporters of the Liberal Democrats fell from 40 percent to about one-third.

And yet there was no sign of a victory for radicalism over conservatism, not even of the opposition over the government party. The electoral system, giving more weight to rural than to urban votes, was one reason for this, but another was that decline in support for the conservative party did not result in an increase in support for the leading opposition party, the Socialist Party. In fact, socialist support rates simultaneously fell—the long-term trend line taking its percentage of votes from around 20 percent to something close to 10 percent. An increasing proportion of the electorate gave their support to no political party, and this was particularly true in the younger age groups. There has been discussion for many years of a trend toward conservatism among youth, but in fact it is a trend not toward conservatism but away from support of any political party. At any rate, Table 31 shows that the proportion who say they support no party has grown to equal in size to the Liberal Democrats' support. However, when this third of the respondents is further probed with the question: "If you were forced to make a choice, which party would you choose to support?" over a third—i.e., 10 percent of the electorate—incline to the conservative party, and it is their votes, added to the solid third of Liberal Democrats' support, which gives that party its clear 40-percent-plus share of the votes in elections.

Table 31   Which Party Do You Support? (percent)

	Liberal Demo- cratic	Demo- cratic Social- ist	So- cial- ist	Com- mu- nist	Clean Govt.	New Liberal Club	No Par- ty	Other; Don't know
1953	40	–	23	0	–	–	20	17
1958	38	–	30	0	–	–	20	11
1963	43	3	22	0	2	–	22	8
1968	41	4	22	2	4	–	21	7
1973	33	3	17	3	4	–	33	8
1978	34	3	14	3	4	1	34	7
1983	39	4	13	3	4	1	32	5

Source: The Institute of Statistical Mathematics, Kokuminsei Chōsa [Survey of the National Character]. The 1953 LDP figure combines the figures for the Liberal Party and the Progressive Party. The 1953 Socialist Party figure is the total for the then separate right- and left-wing parties.

The one-party control of the Liberal Democratic Party has thus ceased to be entirely secure since Japan entered on the low-growth period. Although the desire to continue enjoying the fruits of office has been strong enough to prevent the party dividing against itself, nevertheless the struggle between factions has become exacerbated since events brought its structurally inbuilt patterns of political corruption to the surface. The unholy nexus of money and power, rooted in the fact that elections are so expensive, breeds corruption in a variety of forms which it has become impossible to conceal. It was widely expected that an opposition victory, so long awaited, would at last finally occur in the 1980s. However, in the simultaneous elections for both Houses which took place in July 1980, the Liberal Democratic Party won an overwhelming victory. Dissension among the opposition parties over hastily drawn up plans for a coalition government appears to have alarmed the electorate: voting ratios increased, and many of the votes of the non-party group just mentioned flowed to the Liberal Democratic Party, apparently out of a generalized conservative dislike of change. The dominance of the Liberal Democrats became even more pronounced in the 1986 Upper and Lower House elections. That overwhelming Liberal Democratic victory is no doubt attributable to a desire among the general populace to conserve the present living standards made possible through high levels of economic growth. At the time of writing, support for the Liberal Democrats has increased in the same measure as that for the non-party group has decreased, bringing their share well over the 40 percent level.

At some time in the future, however, there may well be a change in the behavior of such voters if one-party rule becomes no longer feasible and the probability grows of some change of regime and the emergence of some kind of coalition. And, if economic difficulties also develop, triggered by trade friction and the growth of a strong yen, even those who as yet find no cause for dissatisfaction may recover from the aftereffects of the period of high growth and begin to place their hopes on political renewal. In this way, the early 1990s may well be a period when the mechanisms which sustain Japan's conservative politics will undergo change to a greater or lesser degree.

What this is likely to mean in practice is the end of one-party rule and the beginning of a period of coalitions. This will be a step into the unknown for a country long accustomed to domination by a conservative party, and initially an unpredictable pattern of fission and fusion may bring a period of confusion. Given the problems which await Japan as it enters the twenty-first century, one can only earnestly hope that it will be possible to recover from this confusion as quickly as possible and develop a pattern of politics capable of tackling these problems seriously. This will be the decisive turning point which will determine the country's future.

CHAPTER 21

ECONOMIC AND SOCIAL DEVELOPMENT

Conservative politics in postwar Japan, as we have already seen, with the collapse of the prewar policy of "enriching the country and strengthening the army," abandoned the military road and advanced along the enrichment road with vigorous speed. Although an army was created under the name of the Self-Defense Forces, compared with the prewar period the burden of military expenditure was vastly reduced. A conservative government which was able to concentrate on public investment to develop the productive base of the economy brought rapid economic growth, and that growth ensured the continuance of conservative one-party rule.

The beginning of the period of growth coincided with the establishment of the so-called 1955 political structure. This was the year in which new vistas of economic prosperity as measured in GNP were opened up. By 1960, the GNP index, with 1955 as 100, stood at 168, placing Japan as the sixth or seventh in the world, at about the same level as Italy and ranking after the United States, the USSR, West Germany, Britain, and France. The mass of the people, however, in this period of the so-called Jimmu boom and the Iwato boom which followed (the greatest, it was said, not just since Jimmu descended from Heaven, but since

179

the Sun Goddess danced before the heavenly Iwato cave), were so preoccupied with the struggle to acquire the Three Treasures, that they had little real sense of living in a rich country. The country's roads were still potholed (it was "like driving over an abacus") and the buses that ran along them covered passers-by in a cloud of dust. There was a sense of having climbed out of the trough of the immediate post-defeat period, but little more.

From then on, however, the growth dynamic took over with amazing speed. The process of economic development spread from the Pacific coastal belt, creating new industrial towns and giving rise to regional development plans throughout the country. GNP doubled every five years, and by 1970 production had swollen to six or seven times its 1955 level. By 1965, after the first five-year doubling of GNP, Japan was vying for fourth place in the GNP league table with Britain and France. Thus the overwhelming emphasis on production saw effort rewarded far beyond expectation, but so abnormal was the process that distortions developed which could not be overlooked—so much so that even the prime minister who waxed lyrical about the income-doubling process was forced to talk of the need to correct those distortions.

Thus in the summer of 1963, when local municipalities were vying with each other for designation as new industrial cities, and visionary plans for regional development were being drawn up all over the country, the Population Problems Council presented to the government a memorandum concerning "Matters relating to regional development which are a cause of concern from a demographic point of view." The memorandum pointed out ways in which economic growth had damaging effects on the welfare of the nation. It stressed the need for social development in contrast to an exclusively economic concept of development. This was the first time that the word *shakai kaihatsu*—"social development"—had appeared in an official document.

The ideas behind this report derived from United Nations thinking. The original English, "social development," had been commonly translated—and the translation was in common usage—by the phrase *shakai hatten,* as an intransitive concept meaning the evolutionary unfolding of social structure. Now, however, "development" was interpreted in a transitive sense—to *cause* change in society by deliberate policy—and the word *kaihatsu* was used to convey that sense. The *Report on the World Social Situation,* presented to the UN Economic and Social Council in 1957, had stressed the importance of social as contrasted with economic development, and in the 1961 General Assembly of the United Nations a resolution had been passed on the need for "balanced economic and social development." These ideas filtered into Japanese thinking, too: the word *kaihatsu* had already been used for economic development as a deliberate objective policy, and now it was applied also to the social field.

The United Nations had from its inception shown a concern with the economic development of the Third World, and all too often had found that such development was obstructed by illiteracy and low education levels, by the rigidities of status structures, or by the taboos and superstitions of magical religions. Gradually the realization had grown that without proper development of human abilities and the provision of appropriate social conditions, economic development simply would not take place. The idea that provided a country develops economically (meaning, for the most part, provided it builds factories), then man and society would be automatically modernized came to be seen for the mistake it was. It was recognized that the promotion of social development was a necessary precondition for getting economic development under way. Social development became the major preoccupation of the United Nations in the 1960s.

Of course, the problems with which the United Nations was concerned did not translate immediately into Japanese circumstances. Japan was no longer a developing country. Consequently the policy prescriptions and intermediate objectives of United Nations development strategies could not be applied in Japan. For example, it was no longer a question in Japan of securing universal primary education, but of raising educational levels and increasing educational investment; it was not a question of establishing social security systems, but of bringing them to a higher level of effectiveness. And the problem of balance between economic and social development was one that stemmed from the fact that Japan was a first-rate country in production terms, a second-rate country in terms of national income and expenditure, but a third-rate country in terms of housing and environmental conditions. Modern Japan had concentrated on economic progress at the expense of social development policies, and this had combined with the distortions inherent in the postwar high-growth policies to exaggerate the contradictions of Japanese society. The challenge of Japanese social development was the challenge of dealing at one and the same time both with inherent backwardness and with the new distortions brought about by postwar economic growth.

But before the real nature of that challenge was fully appreciated, "social development" was adopted as a major slogan by the contestants for the presidency of the Liberal Democratic Party in 1964, and became a central policy thrust of the cabinet which was to succeed the income-doubling cabinet. The basic purpose of economic development is, or should be, to promote human welfare, but in a capitalist system dominated by the logic of production, the

182

development pattern is, by its very nature, liable to be cruelly suffused by the principle of private profit. The notion of social development based on the countervailing principle of welfare stands in opposition to this, and wisdom lies in maintaining a balance between the two. Underlying that balance should be the realization that when the welfare principle is ignored, the rationality of economic development becomes in the long run irrational, and that maintaining a balanced concern for social development, however much it may conflict with short-term profit-seeking rationality, is nevertheless rational in the long run. But this realization was barely developed, and the colors in which "social development" was inscribed on government billboards steadily began to fade: the slogans were empty. The prime minister himself said: "The production-first ideology too often fails to give its due place to those things that make human beings human: we need urgently to recover our humanity, as it is in danger of being overwhelmed in the tide of prosperity." But there was no real attempt at thorough criticism of the production-first ideology and no real policy transition as a result. The 1967 economic plan was given the title "Plan for Economic and Social Development." The word "social" was inserted for the first time, and social development was acclaimed as an objective, along with economic efficiency. But in practice the emphasis was all on raising the level of economic efficiency to increase international competitiveness. The assumption was that the first task was to increase the size of the pie to be divided: no growth, in short, would mean no welfare.

Thus, in the end, no one showed the courage to challenge the solutions which gave priority to economic development. By 1968, Japan's GNP had overtaken West Germany's to become the second largest in the free world. In world terms, this meant that it was third after the United States and the USSR. The news gave the Japanese people a good deal of slightly uneasy pleasure. Earlier in the year the labor force survey had revealed that the agricultural population had fallen below 20 percent of the total working population, a landmark which was taken as an index of Japan's arrival at the status of an advanced industrial country. It was a time when wildly optimistic scenarios began to be painted by professional futurologists. It was the time, too, when the word "vision" came into fashion to describe forecasts of what the future might hold.

Unfortunately, the English word "vision" means not only a clairvoyant sight of future reality, but also "hallucination." Visions and futurologists' scenarios serve to propagate the illusion that, however much you are suffering at the moment, paradise lies around the corner. They help people forget present reality. Such illusions only stimulated the existing economistic bias and served to speed the pace of economic growth, expanding the economy well beyond what the income-doubling policy had achieved. One of the powerful factors promoting the growth of the Japanese economy had been the high level of government investment. If we take 1970, when growth was at its peak, GNP was three and a half times what it had been ten years before, regular budget expenditure was four times greater, and government investment had increased by a factor of five. The revenue for the investment account was primarily derived from postal savings and the funds of the various state insurance schemes. They represented the nation's savings. And they were used, in the name of public investment, to provide the basis for economic expansion. That expansion also raised popular consumption levels and consumption expenditure, but in fact, final personal consumption as a proportion of Gross National Expenditure had fallen by 1970 to close to 50 percent, compared with 56 percent ten years earlier, while investment had increased from 31 to 36 percent. Compared with the advanced industrial countries with around 60 percent going to personal consumption and around 20 percent to investment, Japan's investment levels were abnormally high. This was the basic feature of the economy responsible for its high growth, a feature not to be easily altered by a few slogans about social development.

And the more the production-first approach brought abnormal success, the more the accumulated contradictions deepened. The deficiencies of the environmental infrastructure became more glaring as production levels rose, and development policies concentrated exclusively on improving productivity continued to destroy the natural environment. The campaign against pollution in 1970 reflected the fact that the exacerbation of pollution problems—the price paid for giving overwhelming priority to economic growth —had become obvious to everyone. The 1970s were destined to be the period when people abandoned the easy assumption that if only economic development were taken care of, social development would take care of itself at some unspecified time in the future. With the retirement of the prime minister who had finally been forced to admit that without welfare there would be no growth, the time was ripe for the paint on the government's "social development" signboard to be renewed.

The new signboard actually read: Plan for the Reconstruction of the Japanese Archipelago. Its underlying inspiration was once again the determination to give first priority to economic development. The 1970 New Plan for Economic and Social Development had as its subtitle: "In Search of an Economy and Society Rich in Human Quality"; it spoke of matters of distribution and claimed that the option of a hjgh-welfare, high-tax-burden society was now available, but this meant in practice no more than that the spill-over from high growth now permitted social development. It did not mean that the basic character of

185

the society was to change. Then, in 1973, the print was hardly dry on the declarations that this was to be the first year of the welfare state when there came the oil shock, and almost immediately arguments that welfare plans must be reconsidered. Thereafter, with the growth rate decisively reduced, Japan began to pay for the years of high economic growth. Moreover, lower growth rates themselves meant that with the bias to economic development still as strong as ever the diversion of funds to social development was curtailed. The future of social development plans began to look extremely bleak.

CHAPTER 22

THE TRUE FACE OF JAPAN AS AN ECONOMIC POWER

Toward the end of the 1960s, when Japan's GNP had become the third largest in the world, it became increasingly recognized at home and abroad that Japan had become economically a Great Power. In 1969 the Swedish journalist Håken Hedberg argued that by the mid-1980s Japan would have overtaken the United States to become an economic superpower. The so-called dollar shock of 1971 and the oil shock of 1973, the year of negative growth that followed and the transition to a low-growth pattern confounded his predictions, but, as Japan somehow managed to ride out the crisis, it remained unquestionably a great economic power. And ten years later, in 1979, an American sociologist, Ezra Vogel, declared Japan to be the number one country and even held up Japan and its successes as a model from which Americans should learn.

How should one react to this praise? That Japan is economically a Great Power is an uncontrovertible fact. Japan, the great economic power, is not an empty facade. But we should not forget that Hedberg, describing Japanese economic growth as heavy-weight development in a land of fly-weight resources, warned that "it is rather like an enormous, fat sumō wrestler dancing in tiny, tiny ballet shoes. And therein lies the tragedy of Japan." Nor should we forget

Vogel's remarks in the preface to the Japanese edition of his book (1979), where he refers to what he had not been concerned to analyze for an American audience—the fact that "Japan's success carried its own costs," which should provide lessons for the Japanese people themselves.

That Japan has emerged as an economic power in the front rank of the advanced industrial countries is beyond doubt, but if one looks closely at the reality, it is a great power with considerable problems. Even looking at the economy itself, high growth rates have failed to deal with the dual structure inherited from the prewar period. Indeed, one might say that the dual structure is one of the things that make high growth rates possible. Again, growth with full priority to the economy has put social development policies in second place; although some of the extra proceeds of growth have been used to improve public welfare facilities, and levels of social security have been raised, the imbalance between production and consumption described in the previous chapter remains unaltered.

The level of monopoly concentration in the contemporary Japanese economy is high, and no fewer than six of the large monopoly enterprises count among the world's fifty biggest companies. At the other end of the spectrum there are masses of tiny firms, and the dualism of this structure is clear. If one looks, for example, at the size of manufacturing establishments, the proportion of employees in establishments with more than 500 workers has increased over twenty years by a mere three points, from 20 to 23 percent. The proportion in small factories with fewer than 50 employees, once as much as 50 percent, has fallen only slowly to 47 percent. Those in the largest size-group—in factories of more than 1,000 employees—remain, in spite of the outstanding growth record, at 13 percent. Compared with the United States and West Germany (where the comparable proportions, as Table 32 shows, are respectively around 30 and close to 40 percent), Japan is a country of small and medium enterprises. Indeed, if one compares the percentages employed at the other end of the scale, in establishments with fewer than 100 workers—57 percent in Japan and 20–25 percent in the other two countries—it might better be described as a country of small enterprises. On the one hand, there are the large enterprises which rank with the world's greatest, on the other are the small firms which still have a very large weighting in the total. Many of these small firms are directly or indirectly subcontractors of the large enterprises. Forever battling their way through a tough struggle for existence, it is they which have borne the main burden of a pattern of economic growth in which those large enterprises have been the central component.

The relatively low level of wages in the small enterprises is, of course, closely related to the pattern of economic growth. The wage gap between large and small firms did decrease during the high-growth period. If one compares the average wage in establishments with fewer than 30 workers with that in establishments with more than 500, the former was less than half of the latter in 1960, but over 60 percent in 1965. And if one takes the next size-group, establishments with 30–100 workers, the average wage went from less than 60 percent to 70 percent of that of the 500–

Table 32　International Comparison of Employees by Size of Establishment (percent)

	Size of establishment (persons)			
	1–99	100–499	500–999	1000–
Japan (1985)	57.3	22.2	7.2	13.3
U.S.A (1977)	25.4	18.0	29.1	27.5
West Germany (1985)	18.5	30.2	13.1	38.2

Source: *Nihon Kokusei Zue*, 1988, p. 226.

189

plus group. Since then, however, the differentials have remained more or less stable with, if anything, a slight increase. Over the last twenty years, in other words, workers in small firms with fewer than 100 workers were able for a while to keep up with general wage increases, but not toward the second half of that period—and that applies also to the period since 1975. Japan, the great economic power, still is structured in such a way that nearly half its workers are required to make do with a wage which is only 70 percent of that enjoyed by the top two-tenths.

None of this, however, is to deny that Japanese workers' wage levels have risen. The average manufacturing wage, while still 50 percent below that in the United States, is slightly ahead of the West German level and very considerably above British, French, or Italian levels. When one reflects that American wages were 5 times Japanese wages in 1965 and still 3.6 times as high in 1970, even discounting the effects of revaluation of the yen, Japanese wages have become high by international standards.

The increase in wages meant a rise in consumption levels which has in turn strengthened "middle-class consciousness," but it should not be automatically assumed that rising consumption levels mean rising levels of living. In spite of a rapid rise in income and consumption levels, if one takes the poverty of the accumulated capital stock into account, the quality of life of the nouveaux riches is lower than that of peoples who, even if their current income is smaller, have been richer for a longer time. Even with a large GNP and national income, so much emphasis was placed on expanding and sustaining the production-related social capital that the poverty of Japan's consumption-related social capital remains unalleviated. Japan's prosperity is like that of a new-rich farmer, still poor in comparison with the landlord in the "big house" who has been accumulating riches for a long time. In spite of the rise in consumption

Table 33   International Comparison of Housing Standards

	Japan (1983)	U.S.A. (1980)	U.K. (1981)	West Germany (1978)	France (1978)
Rooms per house	4.7	5.1	3.8	4.4	3.6
Persons per room	0.7	1.7	0.7	0.6	0.8
With running water	94.0%	99.3%	–	–	98.7%
With flush toilets	58.2%	–	–	97.1%	72.5%

Source: Management and Coordination Agency, Statistics Bureau, "International Statistics," 1988.

levels, the general quality of life in Japan is such as should make a great economic power blush.

I have already made the point that the remarkable diffusion of consumer durables contrasts with houses to put them in hardly worthy of a great economic power. If one were to look at the national statistics—0.7 persons per room and 4.7 rooms per house—the picture does not stand up too badly to international comparison, as Table 33 shows, but the rooms are smaller: on average there is 15 square meters per person—"nine mats" by Japanese reckoning—and a good deal less if one takes the urban average alone. Until the oil shock, the annual addition to the housing stock was increasing year by year, but not since, and the continuing abnormal increase in land prices makes it increasingly difficult for individuals to contemplate building houses. This is reflected in the fact that the proportion of houses owned by the occupier, once 80 percent in 1950, at one stage fell below 50 percent and is at present only around 60 percent. That makes government housing policies all the more important, but government housing at the moment accounts for less than half of the new units added per year. What is more, for a long time the government built only to the "two rooms plus diner/kitchen" standard. This at least means the possibility of a bedroom separate from the

191

living room, but still does not allow separation of the sleeping quarters of children of different sexes when they become old enough to sleep apart from their parents. Much less does it allow old people to live with their married children. In this central aspect of daily life, the residential environment, Japan, the great economic power, still imposes considerable hardship on its people.

And, of course, it is not only housing which is necessary for the full life. There is a need also for the social environmental facilities to sustain those activities outside the family —and indeed within it—which properly belong to the sphere of collective consumption, since they cannot be secured by private expenditure. The narrowest list of such services includes the water supplies, drains, sewage farms, supplies of energy in the electricity and gas networks, parks and public places. In the broadest sense, social environmental facilities include educational facilities like creches, kindergartens, schools and libraries, medical facilities like hospitals and clinics, transport facilities like the road network and buses, and social welfare facilities like old peoples' homes.

As compared with earlier periods, there have certainly been improvements in all these facilities, thanks to the spillover of high growth rates. However, even if one takes the narrowest definition of environmental facilities, the record for water supply may be quite good, but when it comes to sewers we still find that barely 30 percent of the population is connected to a public sewer. Compared with the 70 to near 100 percent levels common in most industrial countries, these might justly be called developing country levels. Sewage disposal is still accomplished in 70 percent of households by the ladling or pumping out of cess pits. As for household refuse, only half is burned and vast quantities are used as land infill, thus leading to endless citizen protest campaigns in the affected areas. Even granted that Japan

192

is indeed densely populated, the restricted size of parks and open spaces defies any international comparison.

This backwardness in the provision of public facilities is a legacy of the poverty of modern Japan, but it is also a consequence of the fact that the Japanese people had become accustomed to such privation, and even when they flocked to the cities did not press strongly for the means of collective consumption to be created. Making their work the axis of their lives, and for the rest retreating to the fortress of their homes, postwar Japanese have shown little concern with the neighborhood society in which they live. If they had been more determined to demand adequate investments of social capital to improve the quality of life, it would have been possible, perhaps, to moderate the production-first bias of government policy, but instead social capital investments were primarily used to create the infrastructure for production, and investment in welfare facilities had to take second place.

Thus, the imbalance between economic development and social development has become glaringly apparent. With the third largest GNP in the world, the social infrastructure is at a level which might be roughly judged to be two-thirds of that of the advanced countries of Europe and North America. That is the reality of Japan, the economic Great Power. The recent charge which caused such a stir, that the Japanese people were a nation of workaholics living in rabbit hutches, may have been a somewhat unfeeling assessment, but it was not without foundation. What Vogel had in mind when he spoke of the costs of success borne by the Japanese people was not clear, but no Japanese can fail to recognize that success did have its price.

CHAPTER 23

SOCIAL SECURITY AND SOCIAL WELFARE

The failure to keep social development abreast of economic development is apparent also in the backwardness of the social security and social welfare services. For a country which had climbed to the status of a Great Power in economic terms, expenditure in these fields has lagged.

The term "social welfare" is used in a broad sense to include both social security and social welfare in a narrower sense. At the same time, "social security" itself, if one follows the definition of the Social Security Council which laid the foundations for the postwar development of the social security system, can be given a broad meaning to include not only income maintenance and medical security based primarily on social insurance, plus supplementary non-insurance benefit systems, but also social welfare activities and public health. This makes social security the broader concept.

Thus the two terms overlap in a complex way, but generally social welfare is used to cover what used to be referred to as "social work." After the war, social work came to be called social welfare work and was then abbreviated to social welfare and became a familiar word when Social Welfare Councils were created throughout the country to coordinate the activities of public and private bodies engaged in social welfare work. "Social security" came to be used in contrast to this in the narrow sense given above. Consequently "social welfare," though it may ideally be used in the broadest sense, when distinguished from social security is a term for the expanded postwar concept of social work.

Social security and social welfare were at low levels in prewar Japan, and this backwardness was closely connected with the *ie* system and with the patterns of mutual neighborly assistance in village and urban neighborhoods. Social security systems were unlikely to develop in a country where it was taken for granted that the aged were to be looked after by the eldest son or adopted successor to the headship of the *ie*. When poverty and hardship were alleviated by kin or by the help of neighbors, social welfare did not become a serious problem. But as the urban population increased and a growing proportion of the town population had no natal village to look back to and no expectations of social security through their kin network, the Regulations for Charitable Assistance of the late nineteenth century became inadequate, and a Special Assistance Law was passed in 1929. Still, however, in the villages it was thought a matter of shame to have a relative—even a distant relative—who was receiving public assistance, and even in the towns to be registered as a public assistance card-holder was seen as proof that one had fallen to the status of the poorest of the poor—joining the "card class" was something that happened only to the dregs of society. The idea that one might seek assistance *as of right* was totally absent.

In such a cultural setting, the care of orphans and single old people was necessarily left to institutions run predominantly by private charities. These were places for people who were absolutely alone in the world, and proper and pitiable objects of charitable works. There was no concept of basic human rights which such people also could claim to enjoy. A large proportion of these institutions were run on contributions from the well-off, animated by the Christian spirit of brotherly love; and the close connection between social work and Christanity in Japan is a significant indication of the extent to which social work was alien to the nation's traditions.

In these circumstances, it was only when the limits to family and neighborhood assistance became all too clear that any kind of medical insurance became general. It was in 1938 that a national health insurance scheme was started. As the number of workers in industry increased, one might have expected growing demands for some kind of factory-workers' old age pension scheme on the lines of the pensions available to government servants, but in fact no such powerful movement developed. There was a general tendency to be content with the welfare schemes operated by the owners of familistic enterprises as a means of strengthening a sense of membership in the enterprise family. After retirement the general expectation was that a man should be able, no less than those who were still operating family enterprises, to rely on the support of his eldest son. Thus for a long time post-retirement incomes were left to lump sum retirement benefits and a certain amount of mutual insurance, and it was not until 1942 that the first national scheme for workers' contributory pensions was established. Moreover, this scheme itself had as one of its major purposes the mobilization of savings for war expenditure through the fund contributions.

The postwar period, however, saw a very big change in these circumstances. In the conditions of extreme poverty which followed the defeat, everyone was so preoccupied with his own immediate family's problems of keeping body and soul together that it was no longer possible to expect the bonds of kinship or neighborliness to be a reliable source of assistance. Hence, in 1946, when the Livelihood Protection Law was passed, the sense that receipt of public assistance was a matter for shame was far weaker than it had been before the war. This law itself defined its purpose not in terms of charitable assistance but as a matter of protecting the right to a minimum livelihood. Concepts of social security and social welfare thus took root in Japan for the first time.

The Outline Program for a Social Security System, published the following year, was also based on assumptions well removed from traditional ideas of charity. Then again, toward the end of 1948, the Social Security Council was established, and its 1950 Recommendations were firmly based on Article 25 of the Constitution which declares that all citizens "shall have the right to maintain the minimum standards of wholesome and cultural living." The article goes on: "in all spheres of life, the State shall use its endeavors for the promotion and extension of social welfare and security, and of public health." Various pieces of legislation concerned with social welfare rapidly followed.

However, the unfortunate people who were the target groups of this legislation were precisely the people liable to be left behind in the race for economic growth, people with very little ability to articulate their demands vis-à-vis society. The consolidation of the various welfare measures lagged behind, and the provision of the necessary facilities, and salary budgets for the people who would work in them, were given low priority in national budgets. Certainly, however, present provisions for social welfare present a very different picture indeed from the prewar period. Most of the charitable private institutions which were previously the main centers of social work now receive their operating budgets from the state or local government. At the same time, public institutions have increased in number and the public/private ratio has been reversed. Most recently the benefits of economic growth have spread also into the social welfare field; the facilities at these institutions have been improved and their capacity increased. It remains the case, however, that they are insufficient in quantity and still leave something to be desired in terms of quality. They are still some distance from providing a welfare system appropriate to an economic Great Power.

The situation is much the same with regard to pensions which are the central core of the income maintenance element of social security. The workers' pension insurance scheme started during the war became the Welfare Pensions Scheme (Kōsei Nenkin), the pensions of government servants were put on a mutual fund basis, and a variety of other mutual funds were created. In addition to these occupational pensions, a national pension scheme was organized through residents' district insurance societies, for those not eligible for occupational pensions. This was under the Citizens' Pensions Law of 1959, thanks to which, when the scheme was implemented in 1961, Japan joined the rank of countries with a universal pension scheme. Even in the field of old age pensions, however, there was no particularly strong demand from the electorate. In spite of the very great weakening of the *ie* system, it still seemed to very many Japanese perfectly natural that sons—particularly the inheriting son—should be expected to take full responsibility for the support of aged parents: hence the reason why demands for a full social security system did not grow strong enough to be politically effective. There were few votes in welfare. Thus it was possible for Japanese governments, until very recently, to concentrate single-mindedly on economic growth and to take their stand on the argument that making the pie bigger was the necessary first stage and thinking about how the pie should be divided could come later.

As a consequence, the pension scheme, when it finally started, was of limited scope. The non-contributory pension,

Table 34 Cost of Social Security: An International Comparison
(percentage of national income)

	Medical expenses	Pension schemes	Others*	Total
Japan (1986)	5.7	7.1	1.8	14.6
U.S.A. (1983)	5.1	9.3	3.6	17.9
U.K. (1983)	6.3	10.4	9.2	25.9
West Germany (1983)	7.9	14.7	8.4	30.9
France (1983)	8.6		28.2	36.8
Sweden (1983)	10.9	17.0	15.4	43.4

* Includes social service expenses, unemployment insurance schemes, etc.
Source: Social Development Research Institute, "Cost of Social Security in Japan in 1986" (1988); ILO, "The Cost of Social Security, 1981–83" (1988).

which offered only small amounts, was available to those over seventy; payments for the contributory scheme could be deferred for ten years, thereby also keeping them to low amounts. All this was possible because pensions were still looked on as little more than pocket money for old people. In this way, national expenditure on social security was kept to extremely low levels in comparison with the other advanced countries: whereas in most European countries transfer incomes equalled between 15–20 percent of gross domestic product in the 1960s, in Japan—though the smaller proportion of old people in the population was one reason—that proportion was as low as 5–6 percent. By 1978 this had risen to 11 percent, but that was still a long way below the countries with ratios reaching 20–30 percent. In a world perspective, social security has a pre-history stretching back to the end of the last century, but it was in the 1930s that the idea of social security as a state responsibility took shape and generally after the Second World War that social security systems were established— and were considered important enough in the advanced European countries to receive considerable funds and attention even during the period of postwar difficulties. In

Japan, by contrast, the slow shuffling advance described above was possible very largely because of the structural peculiarities of Japanese society. And that it *was* possible is also a factor which in its turn made possible the high rates of growth.

However, the structural changes in society as a result of industrialization under rapid growth conditions have brought about a change: now, finally, there *are* votes in social security and social welfare. It was in the House of Representatives election at the end of 1972 that pensions first became a focal point of party conflict. With the change in the law that followed in 1973, pension rates were increased and a sliding scale to adjust to price inflation was introduced. As a consequence, pensions became a potentially reliable income source, and the amounts offered began to compare with levels in other countries. Indeed, they are nominally on the high side but, if one takes the high housing costs into account, are not particularly high compared with the advanced countries.

What is even more important is that within Japan's economic structure, geared as it is to rapid growth, the financial administration of pension funds is not given a secure basis within the nation's finances. The various funds having been spatch-cocked together in an ad hoc way, there are a good many anomalies and distortions. Some of the funds are on the brink of bankruptcy, while others are bound sooner of later to reach that state, as the number of recipients increases, if their present self-financing status is preserved. A general overall review is clearly needed, and a beginning was finally made in 1986 to reform the system, with a new foundation for pensions for all citizens, both male and female. Many problems still remain, however, with the social security system in its entirety. In comparison with the pension and medical systems, social welfare services are in need of great improvement. This is one of the

IOUs which Japan, the economic Great Power, has left behind it on its journey along the path of single-minded growth. How those debts are going to be paid, as we shall see in the next chapter, is a problem of very considerable importance for Japanese society given the speed with which the proportion of old people in the population is bound to increase.

As we come to think about this problem, we should remember that the traditional mechanism for absorbing poverty within Japanese society no longer exists. At the time when rapid economic growth was just about to begin, opinion surveys showed that 70 percent of the population expected to depend on close or distant relatives if they fell into poverty, and only 15 percent placed any reliance on social security schemes. Twenty years later the former group had fallen to one-third and the latter increased to more than one-half of respondents (NHK, 1979a). This was a clear demonstration of the fact that this is a very serious problem, and that no solution can be found without a change in the character of Japanese politics. One way of putting it is to say that, having become a Great Power in economic terms, Japan is now required to transform itself into a Great Power in welfare terms. And that is no easy task.

CHAPTER 24

FUTURE PROBLEMS FACING JAPANESE SOCIETY

Japan's is an aging society. The rate at which the average age of the population is rising is unprecedented in world history. In the twenty-first century, Japan will inevitably enter on a phase when it will be aptly described as a society of old people. The implications are extremely serious. Take another problem: Japan always has been a society in which academic qualifications have been all-important, but the recent exacerbation of the intensity of examination competition has made the phrase "the qualification society" a term of common currency. And with the change in generations we are getting close, also, to being a university-graduate society. How society will stabilize itself when over 30 percent of its members are graduates of universities is again a very big problem.

One might point to many other facets of the probable future which raise thorny issues, but in this final chapter I would like to take up the two just mentioned since they have not figured very prominently in our analysis up to this point.

Postwar Japan experienced a "demographic revolution." The prewar period had already seen the transition from high-fertility–high-mortality to the stage of high-fertility–low-mortality, and the postwar period carried it to the next stage of low-fertility–low-mortality—another respect in which Japan joined the advanced countries. The 72 million population on the day of surrender reached the 100 million mark in 1967 and today stands at 117 million. But, with the exception of the postwar baby boom, this increase has not been the product of a high fertility rate. During the decade or so following the entry into the high growth period, the birth rate hovered between 17 and 18 per thousand, the total fertility rate (the sum of the age-specific rates or the average number of children per hypothetical woman living through the rates prevailing in any one year) was two, and the net replacement rate was less than one. The last figure means that eventually population decline will set in. Later, there was a slight increase in birth rates, which reached 19 per thousand in 1973, but since 1975 once again the figure has fallen below 15 and is now 12 per thousand, with the total fertility rate falling below 1.8, a low fertility level which belied former expectations that Japan would settle down into a stationary population pattern. That the population is nevertheless continuing to increase is a natural consequence of its demographic structure, but more particularly of the marked increase in the average life expectancy. The Japanese proverb speaks of "a human life of two score years and ten"' and until the war that seemed reasonable, but by contrast the Japanese in recent years have become contenders for the title of the longest living people on earth, with the average expectation of life being in 1987, 75.6 years for men and 81.4 for women. That is, indeed, a matter for congratulation, but one which also carries with it the very serious problem of an increasing dependency ratio as the proportion of the population who are working diminishes and the proportion of old people grows.

The proportion of old people in the population is bound to increase on something of the scale shown in Table 35.

Table 35   Estimated Age Structure of the Future Population
(percent)

Year	up to 14	15–64	65+	75+
1985	21.5	68.2	10.3	3.9
2000	18.0	65.8	16.3	6.4
2020	16.5	59.9	23.6	11.3

Source: Institute of Population Problems [Jinkō Mondai Kenkyūjo], 1986.
Median estimates.

The proportion aged 65 and over, which is now 10 percent, is expected to be over 16 percent at the dawn of the twenty-first century, and 24 percent in 2020. What this means is that whereas at present there are 7.5 members of the working-age population to support one old person, the time will soon come when there will be only 4.3 persons. It is no exaggeration to say that it is a serious issue whether or not the much longer lives that the Japanese people have come to live can in future be lived in comfort and security. Settling the IOU inherited from the past—the pension and social welfare problem discussed in the last chapter—is likely to become more and more difficult in the future.

It is in these circumstances and with this prospect in view that one heard until recently arguments in favor of a "Japanese-type" welfare society which reinforces the family and looks to *it* to provide security for old people. In spite of a slow decrease, the proportion of old people who are living with their children or other relatives is still over 65 percent. This is an extremely high figure compared with the 20 or 30 percent common in the industrial countries of Western Europe. I have already pointed out that this is one factor which has softened the demands for state social security, but the question remains whether or not this pattern of provision for the aged can continue in the same way in future. Just as the proportions actually living with children are decreasing, so there is a clear decrease in the proportion who say in response to questionnaires that they expect to be looked after by their children in their old age. The idea that children should be naturally expected to look after their parents is far from dead, but there is no doubt that the numbers living separately are increasing. There would be no problem about that if living separately were the result of a joint decision desired by both parties, but frequently it is simply a forced choice settled by poor housing conditions, and unless there is a big change in housing policy the numbers living apart for that reason are likely to increase. They are already high among the poorer strata of the urban population. When, in such cases, one member of a couple dies and the survivor is ill and forced to move into cramped housing with his or her children, the resulting unhappiness is not only the unhappiness of the old person, but also of child and grandchild. If the advocates of a Japanese-type welfare society are expecting to economize on social security expenditure by relying on what remains of the traditions of the Japanese *ie* (in which old people living with their children was taken for granted), then they are nourishing an illusion, the eventual costs of which are bound to be severe. Even to sustain a so-called Japanese type of welfare pattern we must look forward to maintaining social security standards at least at their present levels and to making social welfare policies more adequate and effective.

It goes without saying that in general those old people who have children and are living with them are more fortunate than those who have none. In the surveys of the Ministry of Health and Welfare, households which are made up exclusively of men aged 65 and over or women aged 60 and over (with or without the addition of children under 18) are designated "old-person households." Such households were around 2 percent of all households in 1960, but now exceed 8 percent. Of these households, one in twelve are in receipt of public assistance, an assistance rate some four times that of the national average. Such old-person households are likely to increase in future. It is these people who are left out of the picture painted by the advocates of a Japanese-type welfare society: they are the people who need pension schemes sufficient to prevent their having to rely on public assistance.

To guarantee pension levels of this kind, of course, would require increased contributions and an increase in some form of taxation to cover an increased transfer from the state. And yet public opinion surveys show that this would not be easy. In surveys conducted by the Prime Minister's Office, the proportions who said that an increased tax burden had to be accepted in order to provide adequate social security was over 40 percent around 1960, but by 1970 had fallen below 30 percent, and in the most recent, 1980, survey 24 percent were in favor of the high-welfare–high-tax-burden solution compared with 40 percent against. The question of how to pay for social security seems, on present showing, to be set for a major confrontation between the generations. As a consequence, people are beginning to advocate raising the pensionable age to 65, and such a move seems eventually inevitable. But if, thereby, the definition of "working age" is changed and the upper limit shifts from 59 to 64, it will be necessary for people to be able to work to that upper limit. And this is by no means an easy thing to achieve, as is clearly indicated by the results of many years of public advocacy of raising the retirement limit to age 60. In 1985 the number of organizations which had a retirement age of 60 finally reached 51 percent of the total, but those with higher retirement ages consisted of only about 5 percent. The fact remains that, however difficult a problem it may be to tackle, the harmonization of social welfare policy with employment policy is a task which Japanese society has to face up to as it moves into the twenty-first century.

In actual fact, the proportion of Japanese aged 65 and over who are still working is greater than in Western Europe. One plausible explanation is that this is because they don't know how to do anything else but work, but it is also because they need to work to live. The total working population, including such people, increased by 9 million, from 45 million to 54 million, between 1960 and 1975. The population of working age, by contrast, largely thanks to the arrival of children born during the baby boom, increased by as much as 16 million over the same period. The 6 million difference is, of course, accounted for by the increased attendance at high schools and universities and the declining rate of entrance into the labor market of middle and high school graduates. Twenty-five years ago, the proportion of the 15–19 age group still in full-time education was less than 30 percent for men and around one-quarter for women. Now it is close to 50 percent for men and over one-third for women. The proportion of middle school leavers going on to high school is now 95 percent, and at the university level, if two-year colleges are included, the present rates of 38 percent for men and over 32 percent for women will, over the years, drastically change the structure of the labor force. In the year 2000, when the children of the baby boom reach late middle age and that age band represents 40 percent of the working age population, they will be of a very different character, in terms of their educational records, from their present counterparts. Whether or not the quantity and quality of labor demanded will adjust itself to the change is another very serious problem which overshadows Japan's future—the problem of the highly qualified late-middle-aged—quite separate from the problem of the old-age pensions.

The figures in Table 36 are derived from the work of a

survey group which has investigated social stratification in Japan. They show the distribution of qualification levels within the different generations as of 1975 (Tominaga, 1979). Average educational levels will continue to rise in future: the term "highly qualified society" is justified in a country where the proportion of the population who have received higher education is destined rapidly to increase from 10 to 30 percent.

Table 36   Distribution of the Population by Educational Experience and Age Group (1975) (percent)

	60–69	50–59	40–49	30–39	20–29
No education or primary only	29.7	15.7	7.6	–	–
Old system upper primary/ New system middle school	39.4	46.0	45.1	37.9	23.0
Old system middle school/ new system high school	20.1	22.9	31.3	42.7	49.1
Old system high school/ College and university	10.0	14.9	15.9	19.2	27.4

Source: Tominaga, 1979, p. 145.

Japanese society has often been called a "qualification society." We have already seen that in prewar Japan it was generally the children of the well-to-do who received higher education and rose to be members of the elite. In a sense, the principle of ascription was dominant, but at the same time the system could be seen as working according to the principle of achievement. And, as industrialization proceeded, the stratum which had access to higher education was constantly widening.

After the war it became much wider still. In Japan the possession of higher educational qualifications has a decisive effect on first employments, and the life-time employment system makes that first job decisive for subsequent

209

positions. The report of the OECD Examiners' Group which looked at Japanese education in 1970 called this "qualificationism" and remarked that it is "flexible compared to a hereditary craft system, but rigid and arbitrary compared to a system in which individual performance over a much wider span of time helps sort people into appropriate careers and offers an opportunity for the motivated individual to catch up educationally and even change occupational status as he develops his capacities." Intergenerational mobility may be fairly common, even if there is a tendency for it to be limited to those who start from middling positions in the hierarchy, but intra-generational mobility is tightly constrained by educational qualifications and as a consequence is severely limited in extent. It is this which has brought such large numbers to seek university education in the hope of getting a degree qualification. Great importance is attached, moreover, not just to getting a degree, but to getting a degree from the right university. It has been argued that qualificationism is really the projection of an illusion, a self-inflicted injury which society imagines for itself. It is said that in actual practice, if one looks at who gets promoted in companies, the differences between people from high-prestige and low-prestige universities are gradually disappearing and merit performance is becoming the determining factor (Koike and Watanabe, 1979). But if one brings the civil service bureaucracy into the picture, illusion is hardly the right word. It is still the case that the university one has succeeded in entering is likely to determine one's chances of getting the security of an elite position in a government department or a large firm.

Nevertheless, there is something pathological about the gradual intensification of the examination competition and the avid attendance at special cram schools from an early age, all for nothing but the possibility of gaining access to a handful of elite positions. Even though, as the NHK's Broadcast Culture Research Institute discovered, 70 percent of respondents think that the examination competition "prevents children growing up naturally as children should," as many as two-thirds of those respondents also thought that the examination competition was bound to intensify in the future (NHK, 1980). At present, even if qualificationism is not founded on an illusion, there *is* a general tendency to apply merit performance criteria to a greater degree, and the ability of the economy to offer appropriate posts to all those with higher education—which was to a certain degree possible in the high growth period —will no longer be similarly possible when growth rates are lower. There can be little doubt that at the beginning of the next century it will not be possible for all those late-middle-aged graduates to occupy managerial posts. At that point the "qualification society" should collapse, and given that prospect, the situation of the victims of the self-inflicted illusion, torturing themselves through their "examination battles," seems both foolish and tragic.

It is clear, at any rate, that the rush into higher education is upsetting the supply-demand balance in the labor market and that this is bound to cause a good deal of social tension in the future. If one adds the prospect of further change as more women come to seek careers, the problem could be very serious. How far it will be possible to change the character of Japanese workplaces, shifting over from qualification criteria to performance criteria and thereby both lessening this tension and shifting to a new labor market balance, is a question which hangs over Japan's future.

EPILOGUE

We have considered the marked changes—and the continuities—in postwar Japan. Most Japanese consider these vast changes as changes for the better. In a public opinion survey carried out by the Prime Minister's Office in 1955, ten years after the defeat, people were asked which they thought was the better: social conditions before the war or after the war. Nearly one-half—45 percent—said that prewar Japan was preferable, and only 16 percent said the opposite. In a similar survey by NHK nearly two decades later, in 1974, the figures were completely reversed: 51 percent favored the postwar period; 20 percent were still nostalgic. Another Prime Minister's Office survey asked about perceptions of the standard of living, the factor which obviously colors people's general assessments of pre- and postwar society. The 20 percent who thought that postwar living standards were better in 1956, just as growth was beginning to accelerate, had increased to over 80 percent ten years later: the fruits of growth were appreciated (NHK, 1979a).

On the other hand, there were large numbers of people —around 60 percent from 1955 through the 1960s and as many as 70 percent in the 1970s—who were prepared in these surveys to agree with statements like: "Japanese peo-

213

ple are too prone to think only of themselves," or "There are many more people these days who think only of their own wishes and interests," or "Too many people are only interested in how things affect them: they don't think of the welfare of other people." More than 80 percent will declare that rather than think about other people, they put themselves and their family first.

The majority of people in prewar Japan, as we saw in Part I, were, to use a slightly exaggerated phrase, "embedded" in their *ie*, their village, or their neighborhood. The family and the community bound the individual with tight constraints. But at the same time, the individual was guaranteed survival and a minimum level of welfare by the sense of community solidarity which prevailed in the *ie* or the village. With the growth of capitalism, economic rationality began to destroy this solidarity and lead to self-interested behavior, but this change was not reflected in the *norms* of the society. If there had been public opinion surveys before the war, it is most unlikely that 60 or 70 percent of respondents would have accused the Japanese people of being selfish.

The great postwar changes, however, while they may have left a certain attachment to the idea of the *ie*, have broken up the *ie* as a social system, and the family household has by and large become a marital "home." Even though the idea that male and female roles in the household should be sharply separated still runs deep, there is far more cooperation on a footing of equality between husband and wife than in the traditional family where the husband was supposed to call the tune to which his wife would dance. And even if the concern to have a happy home breeds egoism, it is a different egoism from the former concern to promote the collective material interests of one's *ie*. The *ie*, too, was once constricted by the ties of extended kinship, by the constraints involved in relations with relatives and other *ie* of the *dōzoku* group. The egoism of the *ie* was not permitted to destroy the solidarity of the extended family group or of the larger neighborhood community. But the modern marital home is infinitely more free of any constraints from relatives or village or neighborhood. Its egoistic and single-minded pursuit of its own interests is given free play. And by the same token, it lacks the solidary support of a social community and suffers from the insecurity of an isolated microcosm closed off against the rest of society. And precisely because the new marital home *is* based on the marital relationship, on the couple as a nuclear unit, even if sons continue to live with their parents after marriage in the traditional manner, the result is likely to be a two-generation, two-unit household in which the tensions which were latent but bearable in the old unitary *ie* now appear on the surface. It was in this sense that I wrote earlier that it would be raising false hopes to put too much reliance on a Japanese-type welfare society. That is why modern Japan must open the doors of the family and develop a new basis for social solidarity.

If one asks where that basis is being sought at present in a world in which the majority of Japanese have become employees, the answer is obviously: the workplace. The workplace has been the one area in postwar Japan where familistic groupism has remained. This groupism—what Baba Keinosuke (1980) calls the mediating group system—was first developed in the process of prewar economic growth and carried over into postwar society to become a powerful factor in the recent acceleration of growth. I have already described how the employment system known as "enterprise familism" was the object of much criticism in the 1950s, but came to be reevaluated in the 1960s and re-labelled as "enterprise welfarism" (Hazama, 1971). The philosophy which underlies it is one which stresses affective harmony in the workplace and the improvement of em-

215

ployee welfare. Though showing little interest in raising the levels of worker welfare provided by national legislation, individual companies have been eager to develop enterprise welfare systems. Nevertheless, the ties of workplace friendships are being attenuated. With the further progress of automation and rationalization, the micro-community atmosphere of the workplace cannot but change. The overwhelming majority of people may still have a preference for a boss who takes interest in one's personal life as well as one's work life, but the changing reality increasingly belies these expectations, and the change affects white collar and blue collar workers equally. Such trends are likely to become more pronounced in future as the seniority system inevitably becomes watered down, and performance criteria and the merit system are more rigorously applied. The enterprise is bound, in other words, to become an unfavorable framework for the development of social solidarity.

In the Japan of the future, therefore, a more open-door family must seek a new basis for solidarity in the neighborhood in which they reside. This is the building of a new community to which I referred at the end of Part II. The loan-word *komyuniti*, as distinct from the standard term *kyōdōtai*, came into general use after 1969 when a subcommittee of the People's Welfare Council issued a report of its deliberations entitled *Komyuniti: Regaining a Sense of Humanity in the Places where Life is Lived*, a report which had some small reflection in the subsequent orientation of administrative policies. It is, however, easier to talk about rebuilding a sense of solidary community which is different from the old bonds of neighborhood, but less easy to do it in practice. Citizens' movements have certainly sprung up and been effective in agitating over the lack of environmental facilities or about pollution, but they were prompted by the sheer need to solve particular problems. It was that which momentarily got people out of their homes. There have not been many cases in which movements once formed in this way have continued beyond some sort of solution to the original problem and led to the creation of some sort of new community. The task is clearly not easy.

But however difficult the task may be, community action is necessary to restore a decent balance in a Japan which suffers from a notable backwardness in the provision of social infrastructure facilities and where the distortions caused by the single-minded priority given to production are showing an exponential accumulation of negative consequences. Social welfare is not simply a matter of building facilities and administrative systems. As current discussions of the increasing importance of community care always assume, the poor and the handicapped need communities. And so do other people: everyone's welfare depends on reproducing the lost ties of neighborhood in new-style communities.

The provision of all sorts of environmental facilities—to help children grow up, to prevent juvenile and adolescent delinquency, and to make possible some positive use of the lengthening periods of leisure—is a matter best handled at the local community level. The problems which the small marital home of today cannot deal with, the problems of the handicapped and of bedridden old people, need a community solution, the development of some kind of organized cooperative care. It is a great challenge to us as a nation to find a form of community organization which can yield spiritual enrichment of this sort as well as recreational pleasure. Doubtless this will require administration-by-dialogue with wide popular participation, and one might hope that this participation in local government will serve also as an education in national politics. Perhaps, by the operation of a virtuous circle, change in national politics would thereby result which could in turn facilitate a solu-

217

tion of these problems at the local level. When such a virtuous circle replaces the vicious circle of politics of the present day, then, and only then, will Japan become a country of which its citizens can be proud.

Table 37 shows the Institute of Statistical Mathematics' findings concerning the Japanese people's view of their standing versus Westerners. Nearly 30 percent thought in 1953 the Japanese were inferior, but their numbers rapidly decreased during the high-growth period to around a tenth, while more than half came to claim superiority (Tōkei Sūri Kenkyūjo, 1970). In a 1983 NHK survey, while 70 percent of the respondents still thought that Japan had a lot to learn from foreign countries, nearly 60 percent saw Japan as a first-rate country (NHK, 1979a, 1985). National self-confidence has returned in full measure.

Table 37   The Japanese and Western People (percent)

Japanese people are	Superior	Inferior	No different	Can't generalize	Don't know
1953	20	28	14	23	15
1968	47	11	12	22	8
1983	53	8	12	23	5

Source: The Institute of Statistical Mathematics, Kokuminsei Chōsa [Survey of the National Character].

But to give real backing to this confidence, Japan must become a society which pays more attention to the fair distribution of the national cake rather than to increasing its size, a society which places full and proper emphasis on the improvement and preservation of the living environment and on the enhancement of social security provisions. One can see how extremely difficult this will be when one traces the path Japan has followed hitherto—from a concern with enriching the country and strengthening the army to a concern solely with enriching the country, until now all the signs are of a revival of the "strengthen the army" objective. Welfare expenditure which brings no material profit and does not directly increase productivity is always likely to be inhibited. This has been Japan's tradition hitherto. This has been what has counted as normal politics. And that bred-in-the-bone traditional, normal pattern has bred indifference and apathy.

But unless we can overcome that indifference and apathy, Japanese society will never be a society to be proud of. Social welfare in the broad sense should no longer be seen as a matter of charity toward a small number of poor people, to the aged who find themselves in difficulties, or to a few handicapped children, but as a matter for the population as a whole. We must create a situation in which everyone can grow old without regretting his longevity, in which women who suffer some misfortune and have to bring up their children alone are able easily to do so, in which the handicapped can feel glad to be alive. When we have a land in which everyone who works seriously and everyone who lacks the ability to work are equally guaranteed for the whole of their lives the "healthy and cultured living standard" promised in the Constitution, then and only then will Japan deserve to be counted a first-rate country.

BIBLIOGRAPHY

Aruga Kizaemon. 1967. "Kō-shi no kannen to Nihon-shakai no kōzō" [The public-private dichotomy and the structure of Japanese society]. In *Aruga Kizaemon chosaku-shū* [The writings of Aruga Kizaemon], vol. 4. Tokyo: Miraisha.

Baba Keinosuke. 1980. *Fukushi-shakai no Nihonteki keitai* [A Japanese style of welfare society]. Tokyo: Tōyō Keizai Shimpōsha.

Dore, R. P. 1958. *City Life in Japan.* Berkeley and Los Angeles: University of California Press. Tr. Aoi Kazuo and Tsukamoto Tetsundo. *Toshi no Nihonjin.* Tokyo: Iwanami Shoten, 1962.

―――. 1964. *Education in Tokugawa Japan.* London: Routledge and Kegan Paul. Tr. Matsui Hiromichi. *Edo-jidai no kyōiku.* Tokyo: Iwanami Shoten, 1970.

Durkheim, Emile, 1897. *Le Suicide: Etude de Sociologie.* Paris: Felix Alcan. Tr. Miyajima Takashi. *Jisatsuron.* Tokyo: Chūō Kōronsha, 1968.

Fukushima Masao. 1967. *Nihon shihon-shugi to ie-seido* [Japanese capitalism and the *ie* system]. Tokyo: University of Tokyo Press.

Fukutake Tadashi. 1948. *Shakaigaku no gendaiteki kadai* [The task of sociology in the modern age]. Tokyo: Nihon Hyōronsha.

―――. 1952. *Shakaigaku no kihon mondai* [The basic problems of sociology]. Tokyo: University of Tokyo Press.

―――. 1960. "Nihon shakai no jinteki kōzō." In *Kiezai shutaisei kōza* [Symposium on autonomy in the economy], edited by Arisawa Hiromi, Tōhata Seiichi, and Nakayama Ichirō. Tokyo: Chūō Kōronsha.

————. 1967. *Rural Society: China, India, Japan*. Tokyo: University of Tokyo Press.

————. 1969. "Towards a Comparative Theory of Asian Rural Societies." In Fukutake Tadashi, *Shakaigaku no hōhō to kadai* [Methods and problems of sociology]. Tokyo: University of Tokyo Press.

————. 1972. *Gendai Nihon shakai-ron* [Japanese society today]. Tokyo: University of Tokyo Press. Tr. *Japanese Society Today*. Tokyo: University of Tokyo Press, 1974; second edition, 1981.

Hazama Hiroshi. 1971. *Nihonteki keiei: shūdan-shugi no kōzai* [Japanese-style management: the merits and demerits of groupism). Tokyo: Nihon Keizai Shimbunsha.

Hedberg, Håkan. 1969. *The Japanese Challenge*. Tr. Sekiguchi Yasushi, *Nihon no chōsen—1980 nendai no keizai chō-taikoku*. Tokyo: Mainichi Shimbunsha, 1970.

Iwai Hiroaki. 1963. *Byōri-shūdan no kōzō* [The structure of deviant groups]. Tokyo: Seishin Shobō.

Kamishima Jirō. 1961. *Kindai Nihon no seishin kōzō* [The mental structure of modern Japan]. Tokyo: Iwanami Shoten.

Kawashima Takeyoshi. 1948. *Nihon shakai no kazokuteki kōsei* [The familistic structure of Japanese society]. Tokyo: Gakusei Shobō, later Nihon Hyōronsha.

Kida Minoru. 1956. *Nihon bunka no kontei ni hisomu mono* [The substratum of Japanese culture]. Tokyo: Kōdansha.

Koike Kazuo and Watanabe Yukio. 1979. *Gakureki shakai no kyozō* [The empty myth of the qualification soiety]. Tokyo: Tōyō Keizai Shimpōsha.

MacIver, R. M. 1917. *Community: A Sociological Study*. London: Macmillan. Tr. Naka Hisao and Matsumoto Michiharu. *Komyuniti*. Tokyo: Minerva, 1975.

Mannari Hiroshi. 1965. *Bijinesu Eriito* [The business elite]. Tokyo: Chūō Kōronsha. Tr. *The Japanese Business Leaders*. Tokyo: University of Tokyo Press, 1974.

Maruyama Masao. 1956. "Nihon fuashizumu no shisō to kōdō" [The thought and behavior of Japanese fascism]. In Maruyama Masao, *Gendai seiji no shisō to kōdō*, vol. 1. Tokyo: Miraisha. Tr. Ivan Morris. *Thought and Behaviour in Modern Japanese Politics*. Oxford: Oxford University Press, 1963.

Matsushima Shizuo. 1951. *Rōdō shakaigaku josetsu* [An approach to industrial sociology]. Tokyo: Fukumura Shoten.

Morioka Kiyomi. 1973. *Kazoku shūki-ron* [The theory of family cycles]. Tokyo: Baifūkan.

Nakane Chie, 1967. *Tate-shakai no ningen kankei* [Personal relations in a vertical society]. Tokyo: Kōdansha.

Nakano Takashi, 1964. *Shōka dōzokudan no kenkyū* [A study of extended family groupings among merchants]. Tokyo: Miraisha.

Nihon Kokusei Zue [Graphic representation of the state of the nation]. 1980, 1982, 1988. Tokyo: Kokusei-sha.

Nippon: A Chartered Survey of Japan 1981/82. 1981. Tokyo: Kokusei-sha.

NHK Hōsō Yoron Chōsajo [NHK Public Opinion Research Institute], ed. 1979a. *Zusetsu sengo yoronshi* [An illustrated history of public opinion since the war], 2nd. ed. Tokyo: Nippon Hōsō Shuppan Kyōkai.

———. 1979b. *Nihonjin no shokugyō-kan* [The Japanese people's attitudes toward work and occupations]. Tokyo: Nippon Hōsō Shuppan Kyōkai.

———. 1980. *Hachijū-nendai no Nihonjin* [The Japanese people and the eighties]. Tokyo: Nippon Hōsō Shuppan Kyōkai.

———. 1985. *Gendai Nihonjin no ishiki-kōzō* [The structure of consciousness in contemporary Japanese], 2nd. ed. Tokyo: Nippon Hōsō Shuppan Kyōkai.

Ōhashi Ryūken. 1971. *Nihon no kaikyū kōsei* [The Japanese class structure]. Tokyo: Iwanami Shoten.

Ōuchi Tsutomu. 1952. *Nihon shihon-shugi no nōgyō mondai* [The agricultural problems in Japanese capitalism]. Rev. ed. Tokyo: University of Tokyo Press.

———. 1962. *Nihon keizai ron* [The Japanese economy], vol. 1. Tokyo: University of Tokyo Press.

Riesman, David. 1950. *The Lonely Crowd*. New Haven: Yale University Press. Tr. Kato Hidetoshi. *Kodoku na gunshū*. Tokyo: Misuzu Shobō, 1964.

Tōkei Sūri Kenkyūjo [The Institute of Statistical Mathematics]. 1970. *Daini Nihonjin no kokuminsei* [Study of the Japanese national character: second round]. Tokyo: Shiseidō.

Tominaga Ken'ichi. 1973. "Nihon kindaika-ron no hikanteki kentō" [A critical examination of the theory of the modernization of Japanese society]. In Tominaga Ken'ichi, *Sangyō-shakai no dōtai* [The dynamics of development in industrial society]. Tokyo: Tōyō Keizai Shimpōsha.

———. ed. 1979. *Nihon no kaisō-kōzō* [Stratification system in Japan]. Tokyo: University of Tokyo Press.

Tönnies, Ferdinand, 1887. *Gemeinschaft und Gesellschaft*. Leipzig: R. Riesland.

Vogel, Ezra. 1979. *Japan as Number One*. Cambridge: Harvard University Press. Tr. Hironaka Wakako and Kimoto Akiko. *Japan azu nambaa wan*. Tokyo: TBS Britannica, 1979.

Weber, Max. 1924. *Wirtschaftsgeschichte*. Leipzig: Duncker & Humblot.

Wirth, Louis. 1938. "Urbanism as a way of life," *American Journal of Sociology*, xliv.

Yamada Yūzō. 1957. *Nihon kokumin shotoku suikei shiryō* [Materials for the estimation of national income]. Rev. ed. Tokyo: Tōyō Keizai Shimpōsha.

INDEX

academic organizations, and familism, 52
administrative units, amalgamation of, 37, 99, 101, 103, 134
advertisements, 119
agrarian fundamentalism, 69
agriculture
  Basic Law of Agriculture, 95, 97
  crisis of, 96
  government policy on, 95
  imports, 96
  output increase, 93–94
  overinvestment, 93
  postwar development, 93
  prewar structure, 91
  production adjusted, 95–96
  productivity, 92
  rice surplus, 95
  subsidies, 95
  and unpaid help, 89
  viable farming units, 97
air conditioner, 172
apathy, 291
  of lower stratum, 68
Aomori, 102
artistic organizations, and familism, 52
Aruga Kizaemon, 54
automation, 107, 108, 110. *See also* mechanization
automobiles
  decreases village isolation, 133
  ownership, 172
autonomy, lack of individual, 43

Baba Keinosuke, 215
baby boom, 123, 204, 208
baseball, 121
bedtown, 40
behavior
  conformity, 41, 42, 43
  obedience of lower stratum, 68
  resigned realism, 45–46
  self-interested, 213–14, 215
bicycle races, 120, 121
birth rate, 204

blue collar worker
  increase in, 20, 107
  and unions, 113, 148
  wages, 110, 116
Britain
  population flow and industrialization, 104
  unionization, 113
bureaucracy, and familism, 52
business
  government support of, 15, 60, 61, 69, 169
  leaders, origins of, 60, 69, 153

capitalism
  development of, 16
  government protection of, 15
  monopoly capitalism, 71, 73
capitalist class, 152
  origins of, 59–60
  See also business, leaders; ruling class
centralization, 15
character, national, 142–43, 144
charity, 196, 198
chemicals, use of in agriculture, 93
children
  care of aged parents, 205, 206
  conformity required of, 41–43
  relationship with parents, 25
  upbringing, 42
  See also daughters; son, eldest; son, younger
China
  clan system, 32
  inheritance, 26, 27
Christianity, 197
cities
  density, 100
  growth of, 99–101
  industrial, 39–40, 102, 103
  neighborhood organizations in, 22–23, 38–40, 42
  old castle towns, 102
  prefectural centers, 102, 103

225

INDEX

cities *(continued)*
  rural character of, 51, 104
  vote-collecting mechanism in, 163–64
  See also urban areas
citizens' movements, 216
citizen society, 14, 117
class
  horizontal ties, 72
  structure
    postwar, 151–52, 156–157
    prewar, 57–59, 70–71
Clean Government (Kōmei) Party, 161, 167, 174
colonization. *See* imperialism
communications, 15
Communist Party, 61, 167, 174
community
  communal assistance, 35, 196
  decline of, 117, 131, 137
  familism in, 52–53
  ideals of, 219
  new style, 216–17
  prewar, 214
  self-sufficiency of, 5–6, 22
computers, 108
consciousness
  changes in, 141–42
  survey of, 146–47
constitution
  peace clause, 83
  postwar, 83, 159
  revision of, 78, 161
consumption, 170–72, 190–91
  mass, 88, 108
control system, during war 73
cooperative, agricultural, 135
corruption, political, 61, 176
cotton industry, women in, 31
craftsman, feudal, 109
crop strains, improvement of, 92

daughter, 25, 26, 30–31, 41
  See also women
democracy
  adapted to Japan, 159
  as gift, 81
  incompatability, 82
Democratic Socialist Party, 165, 167
democratization, 5, 6, 7, 78
department stores, 88
discrimination, sexual, 31
dollar shock, 187
Dore, Ronald, 104
dōzoku, 214

definition, 31–32
enterprises, 51
  weakened, 129
  and *zaibatsu*, 60
Durkheim, Emile, 117

economic growth
  imbalances caused by, 173
  negative, 187
  postwar reconstruction, 161
  as priority, 105, 161, 180, 181, 182, 188, 193, 201
  reconstructing the archipelago, 185
economy, dual structue of, 61, 188
education
  attendance, 172, 208
  continuing, 121
  cram schools, 210
  ethics courses, 42, 80, 81
  expenditure, 172
  failure to foster critical attitude, 70
  improving, 182
  Meiji, 27
  OECD report, 210
  postwar, 79–80
  Tokugawa, 27
  See also higher education
egoism, 214–15
electoral system, over-representation of rural areas, 164, 169, 174
electricity, 192
Emperor
  attitudes toward, 149
  postwar position of, 80
  worshiped, 15
employees. *See* workers
employment
  lifetime, 210
  relations, 50–51, 52
Engel coefficient, 97, 171
enterprise
  familism, 51–52, 53, 145–46, 215
  size of, 153, 188–89
  welfarism, 215
environment. *See* pollution
environmental facilities, 173, 192–93, 216
  international comparison, 192–93
equality of sexes, 79, 111, 126. *See also* daughter
ethics courses, 42, 80, 81
expression, freedom of, 77, 79

factories, size of, 20

226

INDEX

formation of, 160
one-party control, 173, 175–76, 179
rural support of, 164
social development program, 182
support in 1967 election, 174
See also parties, conservative
Liberal Party, 159
life, quality of, 190–91
life expectancy, 204
livelihood, perceptions of, 172–73
livestock farming, 93, 96
living
standards of, 96, 171, 213
westernized styles, 171–72
local self-government, 37, 80, 102
lower stratum,
familism in, 65,
farmers, 64
percentage of population, 157–58
segmentalized, 65
in social heirarchy, 67–68
Lowie, Robert, 11
loyalty
as ideal 15
to state declines, 149

MacIver, Robert, 137
magazines, 118
maihōmu, 129, 144, 145, 147
management
familism in, 54
theory, American, 145–46
Mannheim, Karl, 116
marriage, 111, 126–27
mass communication, 117–18, 119
mass production, 88, 107
mass sales techniques, 107
mass society, 71–72, 73, 104, 115–16, 120
master-servant relationship, 65
mechanization, agricultural, 93, 94–95
medical facilities, 192
Meiji Civil Code, and inheritance, 26–27
Meiji Restoration, 11, 13
industrialization during, 17
leadership of, 14
population during, 33
men, power of diminished, 126
merchants, as future capitalists, 59
middle-class consciousness, 155, 157, 170, 173, 190
middle stratum
in class hierarchy, 67, 152, 153–54
new, 63–64

prewar, 61–62, 63
migrants, to cities, 94, 104
military expenditure, 8, 179
Minseitō, 159
mobility
geographic, 12
and qualificationism, 210
social, 42
survey on, 156
village, 36
modern society, development of, 11–12
modernization, 11
definition, 4–5
distorted 12–14, 16
and industrialization, 68–69
influence of on social groups, 55
outside pressure toward, 13, 14
monopoly, concentration of, 188
motorbike races, 120–21
Murdock, George, 125

Nagoya, 99, 100
national product, expansion of, 162
neighborhood organizations, 34–35
in cities, 38, 104
dissolution of, 146–47
lack of in cities, 136
and mass society, 115
mobilized during war, 72–73
as new community, 216–17
newspapers, 118, 120
Niigata, 102
1955 system, 160, 164, 179
ninjō, 143
nōhonshugi, 69

obedience
and familism, 46, 47
to superiors, 41–42, 44
Occupation
policy, 78, 82, 93, 159
rule through Japanese government, 81
oil shock, 186, 187, 191
old people, 206–7, 217
opposition, radical, 164. *See also* Socialist Party
organization, economic, 165
organizations
communal, 134–35
factional rivalry, 55
familism in, 52–54
group egoism, 55–56, 57
influence of modernization on, 55
vertical ties in, 67

229

INDEX

INDEX

as government program, 185
as spill-over from high growth, 185–86
social relations
familism, 50
subordination, 49
social security, 195–96
expenditure, 200
and *ie* system, 196, 205
improved, 182, 188
international comparison, 200–201
payment for, 207
social work, 198
Socialist Party, 159, 160, 164, 166–67
174
on constitution, 165
as union party, 166
See also parties, radical
society
definition, 12
prewar, 5
urban, 104, 105
vertical, 50
sociologists, on mass society, 116–17
son, eldest
care for parents, 25, 30, 128–29, 196,
199, 205, 206
preferential treatment of, 30
son, younger, 25, 30, 41, 91
speedboat races, 120, 121
sports facilities, 121
state
enterprises, 16, 17
hierarchy, loyalty to, 73
status consciousness, 27–28
status system
authoritarian control, 44
based on landownership, 36–37
breakdown, 81
formal, 27–28
lack of mobility in, 42, 43
See also class
stratification. *See* status system
supermarkets, 88
swimming, 121

Taishō democracy, 72, 77
tax
favoring business, 169
land, as government revenue, 17
and pension, 207
survey, 207
technological development, 88
technology
importation, 107

new, 108, 109
television, 118, 119, 120, 172
tenancy disputes, 64
Tokugawa period
disintegration of society, 13
education, 27
inheritance, 26
status system, 27–28
village, 34
Tokyo, 99, 100, 102
Tönnies, 39, 105
tourist industry, 120, 172
Trade Unions Law, 112
tradition, strong force of, 143

ujigami, 35
unions, 112–13
divided political support, 165
dual loyalty, 113, 148, 166
federation of, 165
of government employees, 166
limitation of, 113
party, 165
postwar, 79
prewar, 72
unionization
international comparison, 113
ratio of, 166
United Nations, and social development,
181–82
United States, unionization, 113
university
attendance, 172, 208
graduates
as business leaders, 60
number of, 204
qualificationism, 210
urban areas
expansion into rural areas, 101–2,
103–4
poverty in, 92
urban planning, 105
urbanization, 21, 104

vertical society, 50
vertical ties, in groups, 52
village
administrative unit, 37–38
changes in, 37
communal resources, 34–35
as community, 35–36, 38
consciousness, 34
homogenieity, 132
increased links with outside, 113

231

INDEX